200

The White Hind

1. John, 19th Earl of Mar

THE WHITE HIND

and other discoveries

SIR JAMES FERGUSSON
OF KILKERRAN

FABER AND FABER

24 Russell Square

London

First published in mcmlxiii
by Faber and Faber Limited
24 Russell Square, London, W.C.1
Printed in Great Britain by
Western Printing Services Ltd., Bristol
All rights reserved

Contents

Illustrations

7

Preface

With two exceptions—'The Ayrshire Casualties at Pinkie' and 'A Ship of State'—the following essays and stories have been in some form already printed in various newspapers or magazines over the past fifteen years. All have been revised, some very much expanded, and three wholly rewritten. Of the last 'The Appin Murder Case', though incorporating material from some articles which I published in 1952, is really a new study, and cites several documents hitherto unpublished.

The stories have one feature in common, whether the subject suggested itself to me or was suggested by others. They are all explorations of byways in Scottish history, from the sixteenth century to the nineteenth, of which each began with a question— Who? How? or Why? Sometimes I have found the answer: sometimes the trail has faded out when it seemed about to lead to a conclusion, but has at least been followed farther than previous explorers had traced it.

Much of the research into these questions has been deliberate and dogged; but a good deal of the material has come from notes jotted and put aside during other work. I am a great believer in two hackneyed maxims—'It will come in useful some day' and 'Wait and see if it turns up.' Serendipity—the rare but happy experience of most historians—played its part in pointing out to me the last surviving monk of Crossraguel Abbey, the circumstances of Barbara Fea's death, and many helpful details of other stories. But most of the material has been hunted down by patient gleaning and sifting in many places. Evenings in the Register House, an occasional morning in the Public Record Office or the British Museum, snatched hours in the National Library of Scotland and leisurely ones among my own family papers—these were not always enough. My reconstruction of the battle of Pinkie for 'The Rough Wooing' began with a survey of the field from the brow of Falside. Visits to Stirling, Inveraray, and Kirkwall were all helpful in various ways. Of the Appin murder it would have been difficult—and certainly foolish—to write without carefully examining the spot where it happened and exploring the surrounding district. And there was no way of finding out why the White Hind of Corrichiba proved so elusive and why the search for her so exhausted the man charged with it except to trace his route and enter imaginatively into his experiences, which required in the end a twenty-mile walk, partly across the Moor of Rannoch, in equivalent winter weather. An historian's work cannot be done only in the study.

J.F.

1

The Rough Wooing

The battle of Falside, or Pinkie Cleuch, or Pinkie, was
fought on 10 September 1547, a day long and ruefully
remembered in Scotland as 'Black Saturday'. In our
own time, however, the date is not fixed in popular tradition
on either side of the Border, and the circumstances of the battle
are largely forgotten. This may be because neither fiction nor
poetry has celebrated any of the leaders on either side, or
because no dramatic results followed it. Yet it was an important battle, an unexpectedly complete victory for the English,
an almost unparalleled disaster for the Scots, both of which
revealed themselves with a suddenness rare in any war.

When the Duke of Somerset led his army over the Tweed at
the beginning of September, he had just reached the peak of a
spectacular career. Beginning life as the second son of a knight,
but having had the good fortune to become the brother-in-law
of King Henry VIII, he had risen to become a Viscount, an
Earl, and finally, some six months before this, a Duke. He was
now the greatest man in England, the uncle and guardian of
the young King Edward VI, and the actual ruler of the kingdom.

He was entering a country which for nearly five years past
had been savagely devastated by a foreign war, largely waged
by himself, and had also been torn by intense and bitter internal strife since the death of King James V and the succession
of his infant daughter Queen Mary. The wind of the Reformation was rising more and more strongly; the perverse ambitions

11

of Henry VIII, the most disastrous neighbour to Scotland since Edward I, had complicated the normal hatreds and jealousies of the Scottish nobles; and he and his rival Francis I had struggled, with contending intrigues and bribery, the one to undermine and the other to maintain the Auld Alliance and the Auld Kirk in the small but virile state beyond the Tweed. The spirited Marie of Guise, James V's widow, and Cardinal David Beaton, able, ruthless, and staunchly anti-English, were France's chief allies in Scotland. But the great Cardinal had underestimated the stubborn and growing influence of the Reformers, and the deaths of the heretics he selected for warning examples merely drew more strength to it. 'The reek of Master Patrick Hamilton had infected as many as it blew upon';[1] and the burning of the gentle enthusiast George Wishart had precipitated, fifteen months before, the long-planned murder of the Cardinal himself by the pro-English Protestants, and their seizure for a time of the strong castle of St. Andrews. Protestants looked to England for help, Catholics to France; and those ancient enemies battled over the tortured body of Scotland.

But now the Catholic party was again in the ascendant. The dream of the greedy Henry had been to unite England and Scotland under the sceptre of his son Edward, and on 12 March 1543, less than three months after the disaster of Solway Moss and the death of James V, the Scottish Parliament had accepted the offer of a marriage between Prince Edward and the baby Queen. But Henry intended conquest, not federation. He forced the Scottish lords captured at Solway Moss to accept the old English claim to suzerainty over Scotland which he revived, and to swear to support it. An Act which the English Parliament passed early in 1543 actually referred to James V as 'the late pretensed king of Scottes' and even 'an usurper'. Henry's eagerness defeated its object. 'On 3 December 1543 the Scottish Parliament broke its engagement with England and

[1] John Knox, *History of the Reformation in Scotland*, ed. Dickinson, i, p. 18.

accepted the French offer of alliance, and about the same time the Queen Regent of Scotland, Mary of Guise, determined to marry her daughter to a French prince.'[1]

Beaton's murder seemed for a time to weight the scales in Henry's favour. But the early months of 1547 swung them the other way. Henry died in January, and Francis in March, and with Henri II on the French throne the Guise influence in France became paramount. Under the Earl of Hertford's scourging of the Borders and his barbaric destruction of their great abbeys, even Protestant opinion in Scotland was hardening against England. The Earl of Arran, Governor of Scotland, who had had leanings towards Protestantism, had been confirmed in the Catholic cause and, as a Frenchman remarked, a French pension had again made a patriot of the Earl of Huntly, who was appointed Chancellor of Scotland after Beaton's death. During the summer of 1547 the Governor had made a small but successful campaign on the Borders, and a French squadron had recaptured the castle of St. Andrews and carried off its garrison, including John Knox, in its galleys. The prospects of reviving Henry VIII's policy of the matrimonial union were not promising. Yet Hertford—now Duke of Somerset, and Lord Protector of England during the minority of King Edward VI—had set his mind on pursuing that object.

But Somerset made no attempt to revive King Henry's claim to sovereignty. In an 'Epistle or Exhortacion' which he had printed in January 1548[2] he showed that his political ideas were far in advance of his time: he proposed the maintenance of Scotland's and England's different legal systems, freedom of trade and of inter-marriage, and the abolition of the names of England and Scotland, the united country to be called the Empire, and its sovereign the Emperor, of Great Britain. With these statesmanlike objects in view, he justified the use of force by reference to the pledged word of the Scottish Parliament in

---

[1] A. F. Pollard, 'The Protector Somerset and Scotland' (*English Historical Review*, July 1898).

[2] Reprinted by the Early English Text Society, 1872.

1543 to accept the matrimonial alliance—'If any man maie rightfully make battaill for his espouse and wife, the daughter of Scotland was by the greate seale of Scotland promised to the sonne and heire of England.'

Edward VI was now nine years old, the Queen of Scots five. It seemed a reasonable plan, and in Scotland it was not only those in receipt of English pensions, to whom the English referred as 'assured Scots', who looked with favour on it. But, as the Earl of Huntly put it, they 'did not so mislike the match, as the rough manner of wooing'. Moreover the unhappy country was not in a mood to listen to statesmanlike arguments, even had they not been so tactlessly urged by force. Men's minds were distracted by the rival strains of religion and patriotism, public and personal interest. There was disunity and suspicion on all sides. In 1543 two French envoys had noted while riding from Dumbarton to Stirling that 'the kingdom of Scotland was, and still is at the present time, under arms; for all the friends of one faction mistrust all those of the other faction; insomuch that not only the nobles are in arms, but churchmen, friars, and peasants travel through the country only in large companies, and all armed with jacks, swords, bucklers, and a half-pike in hand (which they call in this country a lance)'.[1] They had other miseries, too, with which to struggle. Year after year the peasants of Lothian and the Border had seen their poor houses destroyed and their harvests trampled by contending armies; and in the eastern coast towns the plague was, as Bishop Lesley recorded, 'verey vehement', so that 'it appered weill that God did punische that realme with pleague, weare, suord and fyre all at onis for the offences of the peple'.[2]

Despite these distractions, Somerset's invasion in September 1547 produced at least a temporary unity of the Scots against a common enemy. The Earl of Arran, the Governor, sent the fiery cross throughout Scotland—a very unusual procedure for the Lowlands—in the hands of heralds and pursuivants, order-

[1] *Missions of Jacques de la Brosse* (Scottish History Society), p. 22.
[2] *History of Scotland* (Bannatyne Club), p. 193.

ing all men between sixteen and sixty to convene at Musselburgh on the Esk a few miles east of Edinburgh, 'for defence of
their realm, princess and liberty'.

It was a large force that gathered in a remarkably short
time. Pitscottie gives its strength as 40,000, besides Borderers.
The usual estimate is 36,000; but Sir Charles Oman puts it
much lower—about 23,000.[1] As generally happened with Scottish armies, Arran's force was strong in infantry and very
weak in cavalry, of which he had only some 1,500, mostly
light-armed Borderers. The footmen were armed in the traditional style, 'with jack, speir, steil bonet, sword, and whinger,
being the order of Scottis armour';[2] and an English civilian
observer on Somerset's staff named Patten, whom every
modern historian of the battle of Pinkie has quoted, records
the remarkable detail that the armour of the Scottish officers
and men alike was covered with white leather. The Earl of
Huntly, in a gorgeous suit of gilt and enamelled armour, was
one of the few conspicuous figures. Finally, there was a considerable artillery. Much money and care had been spent in
assembling and equipping it and in recruiting additional
gunners.[3]

Somerset, forewarned by one of his numerous spies in Scotland, had expected to be halted in a formidable glen near
Cockburnspath, an ideal place in which to check an invading
army. Instead, he was joined by a pro-English Border laird
with 40 horsemen. Apart from this slight addition, Somerset
had with him some 16,000 men. It was a much smaller force
than Arran's, but better disciplined and far stronger in sub-
sidiary arms. The numerous cavalry included, besides Border
'prickers', a body of foreign men-at-arms under an Italian
commander, Malatesta, a troop of 200 mounted Spanish arquebusiers commanded by Pedro de Gamboa, the Gentlemen

[1] *History of the Art of War in the Sixteenth Century*, p. 360.
[2] Richard Bannatyne, *Journal of the Transactions in Scotland, 1570–3*,
ed. Dalyell, pp. 190–1.
[3] *Treasurer's Accounts*, ix, pp. 113–19.

Pensioners of the Royal bodyguard, and the tried veterans from the English garrison of Boulogne, known as 'the Bulleners': in all about 4,000. Somerset had also a good train of heavy artillery, some hackbutters and archers, and, to support his land force, a considerable fleet under Lord Clinton, which kept pace with his march along the coast from Newcastle.

Unopposed, though with much 'puffing and payne', as Patten recorded, the English army got through the glen and took and destroyed the castles of Dunglass, Thornton, and Innerwick. At Dunglass, after the manner of soldiers in all wars, the troops secured a number of 'brood geese and good laying hens' for the pot. They did not attempt the strong castles of Dunbar, Tantallon, Dirleton, and Hailes, though Dunbar sent 'divers shots' among them, but, passing the River Tyne at East Linton, marched on past Longniddry towards Edinburgh. On 8 September they encamped near Prestonpans and burned Tranent.

Both history and tradition place the English army before the battle of Pinkie along the brow of Falside[1] Hill overlooking the town of Musselburgh, which means that their camp was not in their rear but almost in advance of their right flank. The statements of historians writing from first-hand reports, that the English encamped 'at the town of Preston' (George Buchanan), 'about Prestonpans' (Knox), and 'at Salt Prestoun, als stronglie as they culd, and neir unto the firth' (Lesley), are both confirmed and illustrated by the remarkable drawings of the battle left by John Ramsay, a Scotsman serving with Somerset, which Sir Charles Oman discovered in the Bodleian Library in 1933.[2] These show the English tents extending practically from the beach. It seems likely, therefore, that Somerset drew his army out of their camp and occupied Falside Hill on their left rear for greater security as soon as he

[1] Other spellings are Faside and Fawside: the latter gives the pronunciation.

[2] Published in the *Archaeological Journal*, 1933. One drawing is reproduced in the *History of the Art of War in the Sixteenth Century*.

realized the position occupied by the Scottish army behind the
River Esk. He could not hope to stay there long—Pitscottie
describes his men as 'destitute of victuals'—but in the mean-
time his fleet, which he had ordered to anchor off the mouth of
the Esk, could protect his tents and stores with its guns.

From the old trenches on Carberry Hill, which, according to
tradition, were dug and occupied by Somerset's troops, to the
parks of Drummore and Wallyford where they had their camp
is a distance of about two miles. If the right of the English line
kept touch with the camp, it looks as if Somerset extended his
troops south-westwards to their utmost, perhaps in order to
make their number appear greater. He must by now have
appreciated that Arran's army considerably outnumbered his.

On the very lip of Falside Hill there still stands the strong
shell of Falside itself, a 'aory castell', as Patten calls it contemptuously, which the English had now invested and later
burned with most of its defenders, though its stoutly vaulted
lower rooms survived the conflagration. From about this spot
Somerset must have surveyed the ground below him, extending north-westwards to the River Esk, and the Scottish army
lying beyond it. Looking down today from the same point, it is
possible to reconstruct from the much-altered modern landscape the scene that met the Protector's thoughtful eye over
four hundred years ago. Its principal features are unaltered—
the slope of the ground, the course of the winding Esk flowing
north-eastwards into the Firth of Forth, the little hill on which
stands Inveresk Church on the site of its medieval predecessor,
the sweep of the coast-line, beyond which lay the twenty-four
great ships of the English fleet and their attendant smaller
craft, and the majestic bulk of Arthur's Seat closing in the
background and just hiding from Somerset's eye the new
houses of Edinburgh, which city the English had burnt three
years before. Imagination must adjust the details, and see
Musselburgh—also new since the English destruction of it—as
only a small cluster of mostly thatched roofs; the brow of Carberry Hill, along to the left, bald instead of planted with trees;

B   17

the trim fields of today cultivated in medieval strips; and Pinkie House a small fortalice instead of a stately mansion. Roads, railways, municipal housing estates, and colliery bings must be swept away from the landscape, and the smooth surface of the modern fields roughly tufted with broom and whin and patched with the dark gleam of morasses.

One such morass, the Howe Mire, lay, rather awkwardly, before the English right wing and south-east from the camp on the shore. Another, the Shire Moss, below Carberry, protected the right flank of the Scots, who were drawn up in a position very different from what Somerset had expected near Cockburnspath, but no less strong.

The Esk protected their front, and near its mouth Scottish guns commanded the only bridge over it. Along Edmondstone Edge, the steep, short slope above the left bank, stood their tents, Patten noted, 'in four several orders and rows, lying east and west . . . not unlike, as thought me, unto four great ridges of ripe barley'. The river and the Shire Moss covered their right flank; their left, reaching Musselburgh's northern suburb of Fisherrow, rested on the sea. They might well look confident.

But could Somerset have seen into Arran's mind he would have felt much comforted. The Governor had had many ups and downs in the turmoil of Scottish politics, and his gentle and diffident manner betrayed his habitual uncertainty. He was, in Queen Marie's shrewd opinion, 'the most inconstant man in the world; for whatsoever he determineth to-day he changeth to-morrow'. He had wavered from Catholicism to Protestantism and then, swayed by the strong personality of Beaton, back to Catholicism. He was emotional enough, on his victory over the English at Ancrum Moor early in 1545, to embrace his bitter rival Angus and weep over the body of the English commander, the brutal Sir Ralph Eure. Officially he had been recognized as nearest to the Scottish throne after the infant Queen, for he was the grandson of a sister of James III, but he knew that his mother's irregular marriage was liable to be cast up at him by either Catholic or Protestant.

18

Arran's present position was not such as to stiffen his vacillating personality. He could not feel much confidence in his subordinate commanders. He could not forget that 'ane register book' had been found in the captured castle of St. Andrews with the 'names and handwriting to support England' of 200 Scottish nobles, barons, and lairds;[1] nor that Angus, his second-in-command, had been, despite his gallant conduct at Ancrum Moor, one of the 'assured Scots'. So, even more notoriously, had been the Earl Marischal. The Earls of Argyll and Huntly were as uncertain lieutenants as Angus: only the common emergency had brought three such jealous rivals together under his command. Arran could not depend on Argyll's and Huntly's fierce but volatile Highland troops; nor even on some of the Lowland levies whose absent chiefs, the Earls of Cassillis and Glencairn, were the leaders of the pro-English Protestant party and suspected of being in English pay, and in whose country the rousing preaching of Wishart had had inflammatory effect. Nor could he feel happy about the attitude of these men from the West country, nor of those from Angus and Fife, to the number of priests who had insisted on accompanying the army, bearing a banner embroidered with a picture of a maiden representing the Church kneeling before Christ, with the Latin motto 'Forget not Thy afflicted Bride, O Lord'.

Neither could Arran rely, as Somerset could, on the discipline of his troops. Yet it was essential for him to hold them in their present lines. He was in a strong, almost impregnable position, and time was on his side. Somerset's road to Edinburgh was barred: there were only two courses open to him, either to attack a superior and strongly placed foe or to retreat, ignominiously and on short rations, back into England. All Arran had to do was to wait where he was. But a Scottish army within sight of an English one was notoriously difficult to restrain. The personality of a Wallace or a Bruce might hold them back for a while, to launch their pent-up fury at the

---

[1] *Calendar of Scottish Papers*, i, p. 14.

decisive moment. But other leaders, without such genius for leadership, were often less happy—or less judicious. The battle of Pinkie, like those of Flodden and Dunbar, was to be lost chiefly through the needless abandonment of a strong position.

The small body of Scottish horse showed this hazardous impetuosity, and its danger, on 9 September. The Borderers, in Leslev's phrase, could not 'abstene from daylie skarmusheing', and that morning, along the slopes below Falside and Carberry, they diverted themselves by galloping tauntingly before the English lines, shouting, shaking their lances, and challenging their enemies to attack. Somerset forbade acceptance of the challenge, but at length Lord Grey of Wilton, who commanded his heavy cavalry, drew from him permission to take it up. Grey chose a moment when the Scottish horse, under Lord Home, were beginning to wheel, and then charged suddenly upon them with his demi-lances, a thousand men-at-arms following in support. Home and his men faced about eagerly, and a brisk action followed. But the English numbers and their heavier horses prevailed. The small force of Scottish cavalry—all that Arran had—was cut to pieces. Lord Home was badly hurt by a fall from his horse and carried to Edinburgh. His son the Master of Home, six other gentlemen, and two priests, whose presence in a cavalry action seems rather surprising, were taken prisoners. Of the rank and file few escaped alive. The English also had some losses, including three of the principal captains of their light horse.

Somerset must have been cheered by this incident, but, as far as he could see at the moment, it brought a decision no nearer. He decided to reconnoitre the Scottish position, perhaps in the hope of finding, after all, some way in which its flank might be turned, and according rode down from Falside along Crookston Loan. The monument in the grounds of Eskgrove, stating erroneously that he 'encamped' at that spot, probably marks the limits of his reconnaissance.[1] But

[1] James Wilkie, *Historic Musselburgh*, p. 55.

this merely confirmed the impression he had already formed, that a frontal attack was the only possible alternative to retreat.

The Protector's experienced eye, however, showed him two things. First, the Scottish right was within the range of his big guns on Carberry Hill, and others could be brought down Crookston Loan to bear on it also. Secondly, there was an invaluable artillery position, within short range of the Scottish centre, on the low hill of Pinkie Cleuch, on the Esk's right bank, on which stood Inveresk church; and the Scots had not occupied it. If the English could seize that small but commanding height and plant guns upon it, a cannonade from both batteries would greatly increase the chances of a successful assault across the river. The fleet could assist with a bombardment from the sea.

With his staff and cavalry escort, the Lord Protector rode slowly back up the hill. On the way he was halted by the sound of a trumpet, and turning saw the trumpeter spurring after him, accompanying a herald whose tabard bore the Royal arms of Scotland. With the Earl of Warwick at his side, Somerset awaited their message.

It was a somewhat Shakespearian interview that took place, and might appropriately have been conducted in blank verse. The age of chivalry was not over. Arran's message conveyed by the herald was to suggest an exchange of prisoners and to offer to allow the English to withdraw from Scotland and discuss honourable terms of peace. Somerset rejected the offer. Perhaps it confirmed his decision to attack. He rejected, too, the cartel of defiance brought by the trumpeter. It was from Huntly, and offered, if Arran's terms were unacceptable, to encounter the Lord Protector with twenty men to twenty, ten to ten, or, if he preferred it, in single combat. Somerset very properly pointed out that he was not only a commander-in-chief but acting as head of a state, and had therefore no right to accept a personal challenge. He restrained Warwick, who was eager to accept it for himself, and dismissed the envoys with a proud message that he was ready to meet their masters 'on a plain field '.

Other chroniclers, George Buchanan and Robert Lindsay of Pitscottie, tell a rather different but not incompatible story. They say that Somerset in his turn sent a message, desiring the Scots to fulfil the matrimonial treaty they had formerly accepted, or, if they would not, to promise to keep Queen Mary in Scotland under Scottish tuition and not to contract her for at least the space of another ten years to marry any foreign husband.

This suggestion might well have appealed to many Scots, and therefore, according to the story, the Governor concealed it from all but his most intimate councillors; 'for they were afraid that, if the equity of the proposals were made known, the Scots would hearken to terms of peace; and therefore they gave out, through the whole army, that the English were come on purpose to take away their Queen by force, and to reduce the land to their own subjection'.[1]

Some such propaganda may well have been circulated through the Scottish army as a stimulus to counteract the sombre thought which must have been in many minds that evening—that this day, 9 September, was the anniversary of Flodden Field, that appalling catastrophe of thirty-four years before. A few veterans in the army, such as John Mackenzie of Killin, ancestor of the Earls of Seaforth, had fought on that day; there can hardly have been a man of whom some near relative had not been killed there. On that field Angus's father had fallen, two of the Earl Marischal's uncles, and the grandfathers of Argyll and Huntly. Lord Cathcart's father and two uncles had all died there together, and perhaps on this night he lay awake in his tent thinking of them, for very early the next morning he made his will, directing his executors to order 'mass and dirige to be said for the hele of my soul at the Blackfriars at Ayr, where my forebears lyis'.[2]

[1] George Buchanan, *Rerum Scoticarum Historia*, lib. xv, c. xlviii.
[2] *Scots Peerage*, ii, p. 513.

2. The Protector Somerset

Cathcart's testament was dated at Monktounhall, a small house on the Esk's left bank which was apparently serving as Arran's headquarters, and Monktounhall had on 8 September been the scene of a particularly sinister reminder of the dead of Flodden. At the opening of the Flodden campaign, on 24 August 1513 at Twiselhaugh in Northumberland, King James IV and his Council had passed an Act ordaining that the heirs of any man who should fall in the coming action should succeed to his estate even if not of full age, and without paying the usual feudal casualties. Now Arran and the prelates, lords, and barons with him passed three similar ordinances, two making the same provision as King James's Act, though in more detail, such as allowing the heirs of tenants to continue in their leases, and one allowing the next of kin of any 'kirkman' who might be slain, mortally wounded, or dead of sickness in the campaign to dispose of his benefice.[1] (That such an enactment as the last should have been thought necessary is of itself evidence of the number of 'kirkmen' with the army.) These statutes may have been of some comfort to men anxious about their families, but all who heard of them must also have thought of the only previous occasion of this kind—and its sequel.

Arran himself, during the night before the battle, may have pondered over Flodden and over the strange coincidence of Somerset's words—'On a plain field'—with the same phrase of defiant desire used by King James on Branxton Edge and realized to his destruction. The English were posted now as the Scots had been then. Would Somerset, unlike King James, cling to the high ground and security, or would he too descend, giving Arran the chance to exploit his advantage of numbers?

With whatever hopes or forebodings, the night passed and 'Black Saturday' dawned, a fine, still autumn day, but overcast. Both armies were early afoot, and a little before eight o'clock Somerset, in pursuance of his plan of yesterday, having concentrated his men in the centre of their lines, led them down

---

[1] *Acts of the Parliament of Scotland*, ii, pp. 599–600.

from Falside, more or less along the route that he himself had reconnoitred. First came a body of light horse, then the three 'battles' of the infantry, with guns rumbling in the intervals between them, and last, in two divisions, the heavy cavalry. They moved fast. Their course was downhill, and it was essential to push on and seize Pinkie Cleuch before the Scots deduced their objective.

The long glittering column pouring suddenly down the slope must have made a dramatic appearance, and at the sight of it Arran's hesitant mind was jerked into decision. In a flash he guessed Somerset's purpose—and guessed it wrong. The direction of the English march seemed to be tending towards the camp on the shore. Their stores were there, their wagons and baggage animals. There too was the high road by which they had marched from England. They were going to retreat! And to reach the means to do so they were marching full across the Scottish front. Here was the chance, by throwing troops forward across Musselburgh bridge, to cut off Somerset as Surrey had cut off King James, and at the same time, fording the Esk higher up, to attack him in flank.

Incontinently Arran sent hasty messages to his lieutenants to advance to the attack. The Earl of Angus, who commanded the vanguard or right wing of the Scottish army, hesitated in astonishment to obey the order; upon which Arran despatched the Lord Lyon King of Arms, the celebrated Sir David Lindsay of the Mount, to command him, under the pain of treason, to advance at once. This incident, though recorded only by Pitscottie, is exactly in keeping with Arran's impulsive character and his suspicions of Angus's obedience. Angus obeyed, and forded the river with his division. It consisted of the men of Fife, Angus, the Mearns, and 'the Westland'[1] (Renfrewshire, Lanarkshire, Ayrshire, and Galloway), and included some of the Scottish artillery.

Meanwhile the left wing, commanded by the Earl of Huntly,

[1] So says Knox (op. cit., i, p. 99), who must have known many of the survivors of this division.

24

poured forward over the bridge of Musselburgh. This division consisted largely of Highlanders. As it crossed it bore to its right slightly, advancing on the height of Pinkie Cleuch which was Somerset's objective. Just then the English fleet under Lord Clinton made a brief but effective intervention. The great ships seem to have been becalmed, but a galley and some pinnaces were able to move close inshore and open fire on Huntly's troops. The range was considerable, but the discharge killed the Master of Graham as well as a small number of his men—twenty-five, Patten guessed. The Highlanders, who were unused to artillery, were thrown into momentary confusion, and some of them took to their heels.

For a short time both movements continued. 'We came on speedily on both sides,' says Patten, 'neither as thereunto any whit aware of the other's intent.' But suddenly Somerset became aware that the movements by the Esk were no patrols, no screen of scouts coming over the water, but a general advance. On the east bank were growing up the broad packed clumps of the Scottish pikes. These great weapons, three or four times the height of a man, were carried vertically except when in actual contact with the enemy, because the pikemen could not otherwise have stood or moved in the necessary close order; and in contemporary battle pictures a body of pikemen always has the appearance of a close-growing patch of corn, the banners floating like scattered wild flowers above the tall steel-headed stalks. Below the pikes the white-clad ranks were close and orderly. Beyond the church of Inveresk the Protector could see the less disciplined advance of the Highlanders and perhaps hear the cry of their pipes. The volley from the fleet sounded as a warning, and Somerset called a halt.

Incredibly, the Scots were granting him the very thing for which he had rhetorically asked the herald the day before—a battle on a plain field. No need for him to throw away his advantage of the now slight slope if the Scots were throwing away theirs of the river. He ordered his troops to form a new front. The English, says the precise Bishop Lesley, 'stayed, and placed their ordinance and als their hoill army upoun the heid of the hill in guid ordour, abyding the cuming of the Scottis men'. There were only a few minutes in which to dress the new line, for Angus already had the Scottish van 'in arrayit battell' and the main body under Arran, who had the Earl of Argyll with him, and the rear under Huntly were advancing more like horse than foot, so Patten thought, or in Lesley's phrase, 'with gret furie, almost furth of ordour'.

But Somerset managed to draw up his 'battles': the bills, which had decided the day at Flodden, in the centre of each, the hackbutters and archers on their flanks, the guns in the intervals between, and the cavalry on the wings. Some parts of the Scottish army had a good distance to march—'twa myles', Bishop Lesley says—before they could come to the encounter, but the van or right wing pressed on so rapidly that, says Lesley, 'they almost losed thair braithes or ever they culd cum to the joyning with the ennemie'. Considering that they had forded the Esk and then marched for at any rate over a mile, partly uphill, in armour, the ardour they still retained was surprising. At the last moment Somerset thought it advisable to seize the initiative and check them. He ordered Lord Grey with the heavy cavalry—which included the 'Bulleners'—to charge the Scottish van.[1]

As the horsemen thundered forward, the Scots quickly assumed their traditional formation of the 'schiltrom', that terrible array which had shattered Edward I's heavy cavalry at Falkirk and Edward II's at Bannockburn. The long pikes, hitherto borne upright, were lowered to form a bristling hedge of steel; the front rank knelt, or even sat, fixing their pike-butts in the ground; the next rank stooped, setting the butt

---

[1] Sir Charles Oman, relying on Patten and on Ramsay's drawings, says (*op. cit.*, p. 363 note) that Angus's division was 'a little late in getting forward'. But Pitscottie, Knox, and Buchanan all agree that it was the first to cross the river, the former adding that Angus halted to the west of Inveresk church till the main 'battle' under Arran joined him.

against the right foot; the succeeding ranks levelled their pikes over the shoulders of the front files. Standing shoulder to shoulder, they presented a barrier so formidable that, as Patten put it, 'as easily shall a bare finger perce through the skyn of an angrie hedgehog as any encounter the frunt of their pykes'; and Lord Grey said afterwards that to charge it was like running against a wall.

The slaughter among the English cavalry was considerable, as the speed of their charge and the impetus given to it by the slope drove their horses full on to the schiltrom. 'Come here, loons! Come here, heretics!' yelled the pikemen exultantly as each wave of the charge approached. Two hundred horsemen fell at the first shock and above five hundred in all before the discomfited and discouraged survivors drew back up the hill. Shelley, the captain of the 'Bulleners', was killed, with Lord Fitzwalter's brother and several other men of distinction, and Lord Grey himself was dangerously wounded in the mouth by a pike. It was indeed, as Lesley says, 'ane notabill owrthraw'.

Still, that determined charge had at least halted the Scots' advance. The English had completed their new line, and their guns were coming into action. Somerset kept the initiative and delivered another assault, heavier than the first and led this time by the Gentlemen Pensioners of the Royal Bodyguard and the demi-lances of Lord Fitzwalter. Over their heads the English heavy guns opened fire, and the roar from Carberry Hill was answered by the Scottish artillery, which had been hauled through the Esk. Sir Thomas Darcy, the commander of the Gentlemen Pensioners, was knocked from his horse and badly hurt by a Scottish cannon-ball, though the strength of his armour saved his life; and the English master-gunner was killed by a long shot that smashed the carriage of the gun he was in the act of laying.

The close fighting was very determined, and despite their advantage of the slope the English were again beaten back. The English Royal Standard was in the thick of the fight and very nearly taken; Sir Andrew Flammock, the standard-bearer, managed to save the flag, but left the staff in the hands of the Scots who had seized it.

But from this point of the battle fortune veered in favour of Somerset, who now began to reap the advantage of possessing a force strong in all arms. As his exhausted cavalry fell back, his artillery gained a clear field of fire and began to pour shot into the close white masses of the Scottish pikemen. The hackbutters and archers advanced and opened fire. The horsed Spanish arquebusiers also played their part, galloping up to discharge volleys at close range, for Lesley writes of 'harquhiebusaris baith on hors bak and fuit cuming forduart'. The din of battle was tremendous, and taxed the inexperienced Patten's powers of description to the uttermost. 'Herewith,' he says, 'waxt it very hot on both sydes, with piteful cryes, horrible rore and terrible thunderinge of gunnes besyde . . . the bullettes, pellettes, and arrowes fliyng each whear so thik, and so uncerteinly lightynge, that no whear was thear any suerty of safety.' It sounds as if he had kept his own head well down in a scene which he describes cumulatively as 'deadly, lamentable, furious, outrageous, terribly confuse, and so quite against the quiet nature of man'.

Arran's 'great battle' was also in action, and the tumult was affecting the steadiness of a part of it, Argyll's followers. Pitscottie, no friend to Highlanders, alleges that they 'brake order and began to flee' because of the confusion both of noise and of the clouds of red dust kicked up by the cannon-balls and horsehoofs. But there was another reason for their dispersal. The ground was strewn with the bodies of English knights and horses, and the opportunity for loot was too tempting for Highlanders to overlook.

Meanwhile Angus gave his division the order to retreat. It was no easier in the sixteenth century than in the twentieth for infantry to stand still to be shot at, and he had sensibly decided to withdraw his troops out of artillery range. Moreover he was anxious about the Spanish horsed arquebusiers who were now 'coming down obliquely from the hills as if to fall on their flank'.[1] It was quite correct to fall back on the support of the 'great battle' under Arran. But the manoeuvre required steadiness and good morale. It might have been safely executed if Arran could have covered it by launching cavalry against the English hackbutters and archers. But Arran had hardly any cavalry left: Home's squadrons had been destroyed the previous day. And at this critical moment his own nerve broke. As he saw Angus's men beginning to waver and the Argyll men in his own division breaking their ranks, he burst out with the ominous words, 'Fy, fy! Treason!'

There may have been traitors in the Scottish army to echo and spread that cry. As those who heard it looked anxiously about them through the dust and smoke, they might see the vanguard beginning to fall back and the Argyll men running hither and thither among the corpses that strewed the ground and beginning to hasten to the rear with their spoil. The uncertainty was increased by a heavy shower of rain that fell at this moment and so obscured the distinction between friend and foe that some of Huntly's division on the left for a short time mistook Angus's retreating troops for the enemy. A shout went up from the English lines—'They fly! They fly!' At this fearful moment, as the Scottish army hovered on the fatal edge of panic, two events settled everything: Somerset and Warwick, seizing their opportunity, rallied their cavalry and flung it in for a final and decisive charge; and Arran turned his rein and rode for Edinburgh.

By one o'clock the battle was over. The Scots flung down their pikes and ran for it, some south-west towards Dalkeith, counting on the Shire Moss, which had originally protected their right flank, to hinder the horsemen's pursuit, some west to Edinburgh, some along the coast to Leith. It was the rout of Falkirk over again: the broken schiltroms, the English horse once foiled but now in vengeful chase, and the Esk instead of the Carron to hamper and entrap the fugitives. For speedier flight they tore off their armour, so that the horsemen who

---

[1] Buchanan, *op. cit.*

overtook them hewed them down the more easily. Thomas
Maule, younger of Panmure, who had fought in Angus's division, recalled afterwards that the water of Esk was 'dammed
behind them', perhaps by wagons and gun-carriages stuck and
abandoned in the previous hasty crossing, so that the swollen
water, soaking their clothes, made them 'heavie and onabil to
flea'. He himself, as soon as he had crossed, tore off his jack,
though hindered for some time because 'he had his purs under
his oxter', and thus lightened, but still sword in hand, escaped
at length to Edinburgh and Queensferry. He was more for-
tunate than his grandfather who died on Flodden Field.[1]

The pursuing English were exasperated by the sight of the
bodies of their fallen comrades which the Highlanders had
stripped, and showed quarter to few. Crying to each other,
'Remember Peniel Heugh!' (an alternative name for their former bloody defeat at Ancrum Moor) they spurred furiously
after their flying foes and cut them down in heaps. They would
probably have discriminated between the common soldiers and
the officers, who were worth saving for ransom, but for the
latter's being mostly clothed indistinguishably from their
followers. To the priests they showed no mercy.

The pursuit continued as far as Edinburgh and beyond Dalkeith. The only resistance among this disgraceful rout seems to
have been made by a hundred or so of Huntly's followers at the
crossing of the Esk. Huntly himself, who had marched on foot
with his men and covered some four miles in his full suit of
plate armour, was so exhausted that he could bear the weight
of his headpiece no longer and flung it from him. His life was
saved by the devotion of one of his gentlemen, David Dunbar,
who, as the English closed in on the devoted band who
stood by their leader, put on the Earl's head his own steel
bonnet and, bare-headed himself, was killed by the stroke of
a mace.

Huntly was made prisoner, one of some 1,000 or 1,500 cap-
tives who included Lord Hay of Yester, Sir John Wemyss of

[1] *Registrum de Panmure*, 1874, pp. xxxiii–xxxiv.

Wemyss, and the Masters of Sempill and Home. We have record of a humbler prisoner, one William Batie, who 'wes takin prisoner be George Andersone, Inglisman, and had be him to the camp of Ingland than being in Leyth' where he found caution for the payment of his ransom, 'five scoir of Inglis grottis'.[1] But the number of those who died was something like nine times that of the prisoners: estimates of the total slain or drowned in the Esk vary from 8,000 to 14,000. Patten says that the battlefield was so strewn with dropped pikes that it looked like a wood-yard, and that the corpses lay 'thick as a man may note the cattell grazing in a full replenished pasture'. It was, for sheer slaughter of Scotsmen, another Flodden, and similarly notable in that, as Lesley says, 'a gret number of young barronis and gentill men war slayne'.

Ten Scottish earls and thirteen lords had died with their King at Flodden. At Pinkie fell Lord Cathcart (his foreboding had been well founded), Lord Elphinstone, and Lord Fleming;[2] Duncan MacFarlane of MacFarlane, Sir Robert Douglas of Lochleven, Andrew Anstruther of Anstruther, Sir James Gordon of Lochinvar, and the Sheriff of Galloway, Andrew Agnew of Lochnaw; besides a number of peers' eldest sons, the Masters of Buchan, Livingstone, Methven, Ogilvy, Erskine, Graham, and Ross. The grandfathers of the last three and of the MacFarlane chief, Sir Robert Douglas's great-grandfather, and the fathers of Cathcart, Elphinstone, and Lochinvar, had all been among the dead at Flodden. Few old Scottish families do not record an ancestor killed at either Flodden or Pinkie, and many lost one at both. Seven sons of Sir Thomas Urquhart of Cromarty fell in the field of Pinkie.[3] The Master of Ogilvy's son recalled long afterwards that 'God took my Lord my guidsir and my father (of good memories) from me of five years old, and the whole friends and name all in one day, so was I

---

[1] Acts of the Lords of Council and Session, xxiv, ff. 76, 87.
[2] Oman surprisingly asserts (*op. cit.*, p. 366), that 'the Scots record only one peer slain—the Lord Fleming'.
[3] Henrietta Tayler, *History of the Family of Urquhart*, pp. 92–3.

parentless and friendless altogither'.[1] It was said that in Edinburgh alone the battle made 360 widows. The veteran John Mackenzie of Killin, however, had the luck to survive both disasters.

It took two days to collect enough carts 'to help to erd the deid folkes', and even a month later the grim task of mass burial was still unfinished, for a peremptory order had to be sent by the Governor to the people of Musselburgh, Inveresk, and the neighbouring villages 'to caus be erdit the deid per-sounnes restand in the feildis of Fawsyde'.[2]

The English loss, suffered mostly by the cavalry, was com-paratively small. Sir Charles Oman accepts the lowest esti-mate of only 250 killed, but this is but half of what Lesley, a careful writer, gives as the horsemen's casualties alone when first repulsed by Angus's schiltroms. Shelley, commanding the 'Bulleners', was the only important English captain killed; but so many were wounded—including Lord Grey, Darcy, Pedro de Gamboa who commanded the Spaniards, Calverley the standard-bearer of the men-at-arms, and Clement Paston —that there must have been a good many casualties in the ranks.

They must, however, be mostly Scottish bones that have been turned up again and again by the plough or the spade in the fields between Carberry and the Esk, along with broken swords, fragments of armour, and cannon-balls. Such are the relics of the last battle between England and Scotland (though not between English and Scots) and the last in which the schil-trom without cavalry support proved itself ineffective against a combination of cavalry and missile weapons. Militarily, the fight at Pinkie is a milestone in history. Politically, it had no result whatever, except, as Agnes Mure Mackenzie pointed out, to provide a final anticlimax to 'the thirty-five years' effort on which Henry VIII had spent so much blood and treasure. . . .

[1] *Ibid.*, p. 138. There is confirmation of the many Ogilvy casualties in *R.M.S.*, iv, 1755.
[2] *Treasurer's Accounts*, ix, pp. 121, 129.

His attempt to unite the Crowns of Scotland and England succeeded in joining those of Scotland and France'.[1]

After burning Leith, Kinghorn, and some other small places in Fife, and garrisoning a few Scottish castles, Somerset retired over the Border and disbanded his army. Death on the block was less than five years ahead of him. The young Queen of Scots was sent from Stirling to greater safety in the water-girt priory of Inchmahome, and thence, the following spring, to France. The dynastic union of England and Scotland was postponed for nearly sixty years. Such was the end of 'the rough wooing'.

[1] *The Scotland of Queen Mary*, p. 78.

2

The Ayrshire Casualties at Pinkie

Although there have been two or three attempts to compile a Scottish casualty list for the battle of Flodden, none has ever been published for the equally slaughterous battle of Pinkie. There is much more evidence to be found in the public records of Scotland of the deaths of Pinkie than those of Flodden; but in both cases it is almost wholly limited to a certain category. Such deaths as are recorded are naturally nearly all of men of property, not necessarily because they were the most prominent in their respective communities but because the matter of record was generally the destination of their property. The evidence is either from a retour (the settlement by an inquest of an heir's right to succeed to his predecessor's lands), from a testament (many men made their testaments on receiving the summons to join the Governor's host), or from litigation, the last usually over a claim to the benefits of the Acts of Parliament of 8 September 1547 which relieved heirs of feudal casualties or confirmed them in their fathers' tenancies.

Scrutiny of the records of retours, which are not extant for every county at this period and so cannot give complete evidence, suggests, and other evidence confirms, that it was the Scottish van or right wing under the Earl of Angus that suffered most heavily. We know from Knox that that commander 'had in his company the gentlemen of Fife, of Angus, Mearns, and the Westland, with many others that of love resorted to him'. 'The Westland' means the south-western

34

shires of Lanark, Renfrew, Ayr, and Wigtown, and the Stewartry of Kirkcudbright. The deaths recorded in the retours of men who 'died under the Queen's banner' at Falside or Pinkiecleuch number twenty-eight, and apart from two from Perthshire[1] and one from Stirlingshire they are all from the districts mentioned above:

Fife	12
Ayrshire	6
Kirkcudbright	3
Angus	2
Lanarkshire	1
Wigtownshire	1

The Register of the Great Seal records only seven Pinkie deaths, but of that of the Privy Seal the fourth and fifth published volumes record sixteen, exactly half of which occurred in Angus's division. They are distributed as follows:

Kirkcudbright	3
Angus	2
Ayrshire	2
Banffshire	2

with one each from Aberdeenshire, Berwickshire, Fife, Moray, Peebleshire, Perthshire, and Stirlingshire.

But by far the largest contemporary record of men slain at Pinkie is to be found in the Exchequer Rolls,[2] where the figures give striking evidence that Angus's division suffered the heaviest losses:

Ayrshire	17
Fife	15
Aberdeenshire	10
Perthshire	8
Wigtownshire	7
Kirkcudbright	6

[1] A third from Perthshire refers to a man also recorded under Stirlingshire and Lanarkshire who held property in all three. I have reckoned him under Lanarkshire where he actually resided.

[2] Vols. xviii, xix, xx.

Angus	3
Kincardineshire	3
East Lothian	3
Midlothian	3
Renfrewshire	3
Banffshire	2

and Dunbartonshire, Inverness-shire, Kinross-shire, Stirling-shire, and West Lothian have one each: a total of fifty-four from Angus's division against only thirty-one from the rest. Part of the Perthshire as well as of the Angus losses is accounted for by the high casualties suffered by the Ogilvies, mentioned in the previous chapter.

Further evidence could be gathered from other public records, from family muniments, and from local histories based on both and sometimes including references to manuscripts which no longer exist. As an example, I give below a Pinkie casualty list for my own county of Ayr, which seems to have lost more than any other in Scotland except Fife. It has been compiled from notes gathered from various sources for many years past and, incomplete though it must be, it does give some idea of the amount of evidence available. It also suggests the dire effect of 'Black Saturday' on this one county and especially on the most southerly of its three bailliaries, Carrick, which suffered nearly half the total of casualties in the list.

The Earl of Cassillis, the chief of the Kennedys and the principal magnate of Carrick, was not in the Scottish army at Pinkie. Taken prisoner at Solway Moss in 1542, he had become one of the 'assured Scots', and his name had been in the sinister register discovered in the castle of St. Andrews. But after Pinkie he returned to his natural allegiance. Early in 1548 he was co-operating with Arran, and in December he was appointed Lieutenant of the South. This change may well have been a result of the heavy casualties suffered by his kinsmen and neighbours in the battle, which included not less than seven Kennedy lairds killed.

The list which follows contains forty-five names, of which forty are of men certainly killed at Pinkie: the other five probably were. The catalogue includes one peer, Lord Cathcart, two burgesses of Ayr,[1] the parish clerk of Kilmaurs, who was a university graduate, probably of Glasgow, one merchant and shipowner, two tenant farmers, and three unclassifiable. Of the remaining thirty-five, twenty-eight are barons or lairds and seven are sons of lairds. If we assume that an average of ten followers—tenants, cottars, and servants—fell with each of these thirty-five, which may be too low an estimate, we can begin to imagine the impact of the news of Pinkie on the society of rural Ayrshire.

The list, in alphabetical order, gives the parish from which each man came and a note of the earliest known evidence of his death in the battle.

Andrew, Robert, burgess of Ayr — Glasgow Testaments, i, f. 10

Barclay, Master William, parish clerk of Kilmaurs — *Register of the Privy Seal*, iii, 2507

Blair of Middle Auchindrane, James (Maybole) — Paterson's *History of Ayrshire*, ii, p. 358

Brisbane of Bishoptoun, John (Largs) — *Glasgow Testaments*, i, f. 28; *Exchequer Rolls*, xviii, pp. 470–1

Boyle of Kelburn, younger, Patrick, known as Patrick Boyle of Polruskane (Kilbride) — *Scots Peerage*, iv, p. 191

Campbell of Kingencleuch, Hew (Mauchline) — *Exchequer Rolls*, xx, p. 450

Cathcart, Alan, 3rd Lord — *Exchequer Rolls*, xviii, p. 469

Colvile of Pemont, Thomas (Girvan) — *Glasgow Testaments*, i, f. 23; Register House Charters, viii, 1556

[1] Another Ayr man, William Ard or Aird, survived the battle and was granted 10 merks by the town council of Ayr as compensation for the loss of his horse.—*Ayr Burgh Accounts* (Scottish History Society), p. 109.

Corrie of Kelwood, Thomas (Kirkoswald)

Ayr Retours, 2; Protocol Book of Henry Prestoun, Nos. 44, 47, in *Ayrshire Archaeological Society Collections*, 2nd Series, iii

Crauford of Giffordland, John (Kilbride)

Ayr Retours, 7; Prestoun, *ut supra*, 39

Cunynghame of Aiket, Robert (Dunlop)

Exchequer Rolls, xviii, p. 495

Cunynghame of Glengarnock, William (Kilbirnie)

Glasgow Testaments, i, f. 10; *Exchequer Rolls*, xviii, pp. 418–19

Cunynghame of Glengarnock, younger, William. His testament dative was confirmed on the same day as his father's

Glasgow Testaments, i, f. 10

Davidson of Greenan, Gilbert (Maybole)

Register House: Ailsa MSS, i, 547

Eccles of Kildonan, Henry (Colmonell)

Acts and Decreets, v, f. 44

Fergusson of Kilkerran, younger, William (Dailly)

Acts and Decreets, xxxii, f. 210

Gibson, William (Irvine)

Glasgow Testaments, i, f. 22

Graham of Knockdolian, Andrew (Colmonell)

Exchequer Rolls, xviii, p. 530

Hamilton of Cambuskeith, Sir John (Kilmarnock)

Glasgow Testaments, i, ff. 12–13; Acts and Decreets, iii, f. 46

Hamilton in Bogend, James (Tarbolton)

Register of the Privy Seal, iv, 1398

Hunter of Hunterstoun, Mungo (Kilbride)

Ayr Retours, 8

Kennedy of Coiff, Thomas (Kirkoswald), brother to the Earl of Cassillis, 'according to some accounts'

Scots Peerage, ii, p. 465

Kennedy of Auchincrosh, Thomas (Ballantrae)

Register House: Bargany MSS (Auchincrosh writs)

Kennedy of Balhamish, Andrew (Colmonell)

Acts and Decreets, iv, ff. 340–1

Kennedy of Balmaclanachan, Gilbert (Dailly)

Glasgow Testaments, i, ff. 11–12

Kennedy of Bennan, John (Ballantrae)

Prestoun, 45; Register House: Bennan MSS, 15

Kennedy of Bennan, younger, David

Paterson, i, p. 250

Kennedy of Kirkmichael, John (Kirkmichael)

Prestoun, 36

Kennedy in Little Smithston, Thomas (Maybole), second son of Thomas Kennedy of Ardmillan

Acts of the Lords of Council and Session, xxv, f. 108

Kennedy of Pinwherry, William (Colmonell)

Acts and Decreets, iii, f. 368

McAlexander of Corseclays, George (Colmonell)

Exchequer Rolls, xviii, p. 500

McCalman in Little Bennan, Gilbert (Ballantrae)

Register House: Bennan MSS, 9

McCrindle of Barneill, younger, Mungo (Girvan)

Register of the Privy Seal, iv, 1711

McIlvane of Grimmet, Gilbert (Maybole)

Ayr Retours, 1

Montfod of Montfod, James (Ardrossan)

Ayr Retours, 3; Prestoun, 15

Montgomerie, Hew, fourth son of the 1st Earl of Eglinton

Paterson, ii, p. 235

Montgomerie of Langschaw, younger, John (Stewarton)

Acts of the Lords of Council and Session, xxiv, f. 68

Mure of Cloncaird, Patrick (Kirkmichael)

Register House: MS note by Dr. J. Maitland Thomson (authority not traced)

Mure of Park, Bernard (Tarbolton)   *Ayr Retours*, 6; Prestoun, 29

Mure of Rowallan, Mungo (Kilmarnock)   Prestoun, 27

Nesbitt, William, burgess of Ayr   Glasgow Testaments, i, f. 30

Rankin of Scheild, Laurence (Ochiltree)   Prestoun, 1

Reid, Thomas, baron-officer to John Blair of Blair (Dalry)   Pitcairn's *Criminal Trials in Scotland*, i, pp. 51, 55–56

Scot [Christian name perished] (Irvine)   Glasgow Testaments, i, f. 21

Wilson, Cuthbert (Irvine)   Glasgow Testaments, i, ff. 42–3

3

The Queen in Ayrshire

On Tuesday, 3 July 1956, Queen Elizabeth II, accompanied by the Duke of Edinburgh, paid an official visit to Ayrshire. 'Visit' is the rather inept word habitually used nowadays when the Sovereign appears anywhere outside her capital, even when she is in residence at the Palace of Holyroodhouse which has been the home of her family for many generations longer than Buckingham Palace. In former times an official journey by a reigning monarch through one part or another of the kingdom was known as a 'progress'. Its purpose might be to dispense justice or to suppress rebellion; it was more often to change residence from one palace or castle to another, and at the same time to consume such of the royal revenues as were rendered in the form of food and drink; it was sometimes to escape from the insanitary conditions of a city or to remove to a safe distance from another outbreak of 'the pest'.

But the modern monarchs of Great Britain, who have been more truly the servants of their people than almost any of their predecessors, make progresses for other reasons; to inspect and encourage new enterprises in industry, agriculture, engineering, social services, and occasionally the arts; to familiarize themselves with provinces of their realm to which official duties have not as yet taken them; and to allow their subjects the actual sight of themselves for which no picture, even though modern science can make it both move and speak, can ever be an altogether acceptable substitute.

Queen Victoria began this modern style of progress. King George V and King George VI continued and extended it. Queen Elizabeth II has done the same, and has moreover visited far corners of her kingdom to which few and in some cases none of her royal ancestors ever penetrated.

The Queen's progress through Ayrshire, long hoped for and eagerly awaited by its people, was all too brief, lasting some nine hours of a single summer day. It embraced, naturally, the more populous parts of the county, the industrialized districts of Cunningham and Kyle; and she passed through only the northern fringe of the ancient earldom of Carrick, the home of her ancestor King Robert Bruce and the hereditary appanage of her son the young Duke of Rothesay (not yet created Prince of Wales). But it was a well-filled day, during which Her Majesty managed to visit and receive the official greetings of most of the burghs of Ayrshire. There was some dry complaint that she saw 'nothing but provosts and pitheads', and indeed she could see little of the county's rural scenery, the winding, wooded valleys, the broad pastures, the great hills ribbed with drystane dykes that sweep away to the east and south—the essential Ayrshire which centuries of history have hardly changed. But she did in her crowded hours see more of the county and its people than did the last sovereign to make an official progress through Ayrshire, nearly four hundred years before hers.

In the long interval between there had been, it is true, a few brief visits by royal personages, but they were not progresses. During the Second World War, King George VI, under the conditions of secrecy necessary at that time, inspected some of his troops who were being trained in Ayrshire, and some years earlier, while he was still Duke of York, laid the foundation stone of the new County Buildings in Ayr. King Edward VIII, as Prince of Wales, once spent part of a November day in Ayrshire, out with the Eglinton Hunt. But though Queen Victoria was once off the coast in the royal yacht she never visited the county; neither did the son and grandson who succeeded her.

Of the House of Hanover, George IV was the only sovereign who set foot in Scotland at all, and he was never outside the Lothians. Before him there is a long gap back to Charles II's reign. His brother James, Duke of York and Albany, afterwards King James VII, held state for a few months in Edinburgh as the King's Commissioner to the Parliament of Scotland in 1680–1, but he was never in Ayrshire; and the King's own brief and troubled residence in his northern kingdom in 1650 and 1651 had included no visit to the south-west. Charles I, born in Dunfermline, left Scotland as a boy, and after his succession to the English and Scottish Crowns visited it only in 1633 for his coronation and in 1641, and was never nearer to Ayr than Linlithgow. His father James VI in 1598 proposed to take ship from Ayr to Kintyre on an expedition to restore order among his turbulent subjects in the West Highlands. But though 'his majesteis progres to Kintyre' led him to spend a few days at the castle of Sorn on the River Ayr he apparently went no further west,[1] and his expedition petered out.

And so, searching backwards, we come to the year 1563 and the month of August, when Mary, Queen of Scots, made her progress through Ayrshire and spent not one day but ten among her Ayrshire subjects. This was the last royal progress through the county till that of her descendant in the thirteenth degree, Queen Elizabeth II, in 1956.

Queen Mary's progress followed a period which by the standards of her reign had been fairly peaceful but had not been without some anxieties. Huntly's rebellion of the previous year had been officially concluded, so to speak, by the formal forfeiture on 28 May of Huntly himself (already dead) and Sutherland. Parliament had met, for the first time since the Queen's return to Scotland two years before. The burghs had complained bitterly to it of the heavy import duties levied by the Danes, which were crippling the Scottish Baltic trade, and an embassy to the King of Denmark on the subject had been

[1] Treasurer's Accounts (unprinted), 1597–8, ff. 87–93.

43

despatched and returned without effect. The matter of the Queen's second marriage, not to be resolved till she wedded her cousin Lord Darnley two years later, had been agitating not only the courts of England and Spain but Edinburgh itself. The notion of the Queen's marrying a Spanish prince, which it had become known that she was entertaining, was highly unpopular in Scotland. Before Parliament rose on 6 June, John Knox, in a sermon preached 'before the most part of the nobility', had spoken out with characteristic bluntness against any marriage of the Queen of Scots to 'an infidel—and all Papists', he added, 'are infidels'. Summoned to the presence of his indignant sovereign, he had reduced her, by his own account, to an 'inordinate passion' of tears.[1]

Not unnaturally the Queen, who was not yet 21 years old, chose to make her summer progress through the territories of nobles friendly and loyal to her and not likely to plague her with unwelcome advice or to insult her religion: the Earls of Argyll, Eglinton, and Cassillis, the Master of Maxwell (afterwards Lord Herries), and Lord Somerville. Her route took her through a wide quarter of her realm which she had never yet viewed. It made a great circle through the west and south-west, by Stirlingshire, Glasgow, and Dunbartonshire into Argyll, thence through Ayrshire and Galloway into Dumfriesshire, and back to Craigmillar near Edinburgh by way of Crawfordjohn, Peebles, Borthwick, Dalhousie, and Roslin.

Buchanan's statement that 'the rest of the summer the Queen gave up to hunting in Atholl' is either sheer invention or a confusion with the great hunt in Atholl that she witnessed the following year.[2] The journey was indeed something of a holiday tour, but not altogether. The Registers of the Great Seal and Privy Seal show that the Queen transacted a certain amount of official business during her travels, even at places so remote

[1] *John Knox's History of the Reformation in Scotland*, ed. Dickinson, ii, pp. 80–4.
[2] W. A. Gatherer, *The Tyrannous Reign of Mary Stewart* (*George Buchanan's Account*), p. 80.

from her capital as Inveraray and St. Mary's Isle; and she held a meeting of her Privy Council in Glasgow on 8 July and another in Dumfries on 20 August, the last being to consider the reply to a letter of 19 August from the English Warden of the Middle Marches, written from Carlisle.[1] But her progress through Ayrshire had nothing to interrupt whatever pleasure it gave her.

She travelled almost wholly along the coast, scarcely ever out of sight of the sea. There were no more roads in that region than anywhere else at that time, but there were bridges over the rivers of Irvine, Ayr, Doon, and Girvan near their mouths; and there were several places, at convenient distances apart, fit for lodging a Queen and her train. The cool breezes off the sea would make riding over the short, springy turf pleasant in the August days. Besides, the country inland, especially in Carrick, was thickly wooded, and in many places boggy, with numerous waters to be crossed.

We do not know exactly who accompanied the Queen, nor, since the Lord Treasurer's accounts for the year 1563 have not survived, have we any details of her clothes and baggage. She travelled, at any rate, with only a small attendance, for their transport consisted of but eighteen horses and six baggage mules. This we know from the stabling accounts kept by her French equerry,[2] who recorded where she spent each day and night and the costs of lodging the animals. But the royal party must have often included a fluid following of local notables. At Irvine and Ayr the magistrates would meet the Queen at their burgh boundaries and escort her until she left them; and the several nobles who were her hosts would accompany her, each through his own lands. The local barons, lairds, and gentlemen, too, would ride intermittently in the Queen's train, perhaps to show their loyalty, perhaps hoping for favours, perhaps just to see and be seen, each with his little

[1] *Privy Council Register*, i, pp. 241, 243–4.
[2] In H.M. General Register House: partly printed, edited by Sir Herbert Maxwell, in *Scottish Historical Review*, xviii, pp. 5–7.

knot of attendant kinsmen and servants trailing respectfully in the rear. There would be Montgomeries and Cunninghams, Boyles and Mures, in the north; Craufurds, Campbells, and Wallaces in Kyle; and throughout Carrick a preponderance of Kennedys, with Fergussons, Boyds, Cathcarts, and more Mures and Craufurds.

The tall young Queen, who loved riding and gaiety, must have been the centre all the way of a cheerful and carefree company. There was apparently no public business to be considered on this part of her journey; and in those days sovereigns seldom had to go out of their way to display themselves to their subjects—who were none the less at perfect liberty to come and watch them pass by. No doubt there were cheers and blessings and waving bonnets. But there must have been also some dark looks and surly mutterings in the background. The Queen had many, perhaps a majority of Papists in her train; and, as Knox recorded disapprovingly, she 'had her mass' at each house where she stayed. Knox had preached in Kyle the previous autumn, and George Hay at the same time 'with great fruit in all the churches of Carrick'.[1] Under the influence of these powerful preachers, seventy-eight Ayrshire noblemen, barons, and lairds had signed a covenant in Ayr on 4 September to maintain the preaching of the Gospel and the ministry, and to assist 'the hoill body of the Protestantis within this realme'.[2] These eminent men and those whom they represented must have balanced their pleasure at the sight of their young Queen with suspicions of the policy she was pursuing: well justified too, since earlier this year she had been writing to the Pope that she would do all in her power to make her subjects obey the decrees of the Council of Trent, 'if God, by his grace, is able to reduce and destroy the heresies'.

Whatever enthusiasm, therefore, was shown by the people in Irvine, Ayr, and elsewhere where the Queen passed was probably not quite whole-hearted. The attendant throng of

[1] Knox, *ut cit.*, ii, p. 55.
[2] James King Hewison, *The Covenanters*, i, pp. 54–5.

gentlemen, too, can have been by no means always in harmony, and some groups would be avoiding each other for other than religious reasons. There was no love lost, for instance, between the Montgomeries and the Cunninghams; and in Carrick there was 'deidlie feid and inimitie' between the Kennedys who adhered to the Earl of Cassillis and the Craufurds of Camlarg, on account of 'the hurting and wounding' a few months before of one 'Hary Kennedy *alias* Mady'.[1] The Craufurds also had a smouldering dispute of many years' standing with the Fergussons of Kilkerran, which broke out into open and scandalous violence less than a year after the Queen's progress.[2] Further south still, Adam Boyd of Penkill cannot have been on speaking terms with James Eccles of that ilk, the laird of Kildonan, who had failed to pay his rent for the year 1562 for his tenancy of Boyd's lands of Trochraig and had also refused to remove from them at last Whitsunday though lawfully warned to do so. The two were at this time pursuing each other by action and counter-action in the Court of Session.[3]

The Queen slept for her first night in Ayrshire, 31 July, at Lord Sempill's castle of Southannan, for she had crossed the Firth of Clyde that day from Dunoon after her journey through Argyll. Lord Sempill, an elderly man, was a Roman Catholic. His illegitimate son John later married one of the Queen's Maries, Mary Livingstone: perhaps this was the occasion when the couple first met.

Only a few stones are left of Southannan, and there is no trace today of the Eglinton Castle where the Queen spent her next night in Ayrshire, 1 August. Here she was the Earl of Eglinton's guest, and the stabling of her horses and mules cost, as the equerry noted, '*neant*' (nothing). Eglinton, some 30 years of age, was an old acquaintance, for he had been one of the

[1] Acts and Decreets, xxx, ff. 358–9.

[2] Pitcairn's *Criminal Trials in Scotland*, i, pp. *456–8; *Calendar of Scottish Papers*, ii, p. 76.

[3] Acts and Decreets, xxv, ff. 118–19; xxvi, ff. 241–2; xxvii, f. 274; xxviii, ff. 145–6, 266, 400.

nobles who had gone over to France in 1561 to escort the Queen back to her own country. She stayed with him till after dinner on 2 August, and in the afternoon rode south through Irvine, and reached Ayr in time for supper. There is nothing to confirm the tradition in Irvine that she stayed in the Seagate Castle there. She certainly spent no night in the town, and the local historian thinks it unlikely that the building itself was erected till a year or two after her progress.[1]

It was an easy ride to Ayr, through almost flat country. Over the Auld Brig and by the High Street, the Queen entered the old burgh where she was to stay for two nights. Nothing of the 'Auld Ayr' she saw remains today but the tower of St. John's Church, the bridge, and 'the Sheriff's lodging'—the town house of Sir Matthew Campbell of Loudoun, hereditary Sheriff of Ayr, known today as Loudoun Hall and recently restored to something of its original appearance. As the extant burgh accounts have a gap at this date, we do not know how Ayr received the Queen. Certainly there would be a 'propine' of wine and sweetmeats offered by the magistrates at the least. There is no record of where the Queen and her train stayed. Sir Herbert Maxwell conjectured that it was in the monastery of St. John—but no such monastery ever existed. Their lodgings were probably in private houses, and were possibly hired, for the Queen's equerry had to pay for oats and straw for the horses and mules, just over £19. But the Sheriff may have had the honour of lodging the Queen herself.

After dinner on 4 August the Queen passed on to Dunure. When over the Doon, crossing by the high single-arched bridge that still stands, she was in the Earl of Cassillis's territory—'a barrant cuntree but for bestiall', an English spy reported contemptuously about this time, adding, not very accurately, 'The people for the moste part speketht Erishe'.[2]

At Dunure ('a fare castell, not stronge nor worthy fortifying',

[1] A. F. McJannet, *Royal Burgh of Irvine*, p. 99.
[2] *Archaeological and Historical Collections relating to Ayr and Wigton*, iv, pp. 17–19.

thought the Englishman), the Queen remained for three nights, her longest stay in Ayrshire. Cassillis, her host, 'that young papist erle', was only a few months older than she, and perhaps took her out hawking at grouse, partridges, and hares on the green hillsides overlooking the firth with their splendid view of silver sea and blue islands backed by the three pointed peaks of Arran and the far grey outline of Kintyre. Some visitors she certainly received here. Among them may have been Cassillis's uncle, the pious and earnest Abbot Quintin Kennedy of Crossraguel, a devoted champion of the Roman Church who the previous year had challenged John Knox to dispute with him on the Scriptural justification of the Mass, and held his own during three days of argument in Maybole. He still lived in his abbey, a bare six miles distant from Dunure. Other visitors probably included some of Cassillis's principal clansmen such as Thomas Kennedy of Bargany, who was to be the Queen's host later, and John Kennedy of Blairquhan. 'These tuo,' the English spy reported, 'be nothing inferior in leving to therle of Cassills'; and there were other Kennedy lairds also who would have felt themselves slighted if their young chief had not presented them to the Queen.

One small gathering of local lairds, at least, there must have been at Dunure during the Queen's stay there. While in Ayrshire she issued two precepts under her Privy Seal; the first at Southannan, the second at Dunure. The latter (wrongly dated in the Register 15 August, by which day the Queen was in Wigtownshire) was for a charter to Robert Wallace, son and apparent heir of Hew Wallace of Carnell, granting him some lands in Kyle-Stewart. These lands had been held previously by two Kennedy sisters, Gelis Kennedy, widow of John Grierson of Lag, and Jonet Kennedy, wife of George Kennedy of Barclanachan, who resigned them in Robert's favour.[1] The formal ceremony of resignation 'by staff and baston' into the superior's hands was usually performed to a deputy when the

[1] They were sisters and heirs of umquhile John Kennedy of Culzean (Acts and Decreets, xxiv, f. 136).

superior was the sovereign or a great noble. But in this case the record shows that the resignation was made *apud Dunnure*, and *in manibus S.D.N. regine*: the opportunity was taken to enact this little ceremony, symbolic of feudal duty, to the Sovereign in person. Kyle-Stewart, like Carrick, is an appanage of the Prince and Steward of Scotland, who is also Duke of Rothesay and Earl of Carrick, and the Queen, having as yet no heir, was acting *tanquam Princeps* and at this moment resident in the Stewartry lands; so the moment was felicitously chosen. The resignation was actually performed on the ladies' behalf by procurators, who were probably local lairds, and it may be assumed that several Kennedys and Wallaces were present.[1]

Dunure, though not thought 'worthy fortifying', perhaps because at that date it possessed no harbour, was superbly sited on a high rocky headland overlooking the firth and a wide stretch of shore, and the view as well as the company may have tempted Queen Mary to linger there. But on 7 August she continued her journey, after dinner was over, along the coast to Ardmillan, a ride of something over twenty miles. The high rectangular tower of Ardmillan was snugly tucked under a steep hill facing the sea, a short distance beyond the Water of Girvan's mouth, and here the Queen's host was 'the Gudeman of Ardmillan', John Kennedy, a middle-aged cousin of the laird of Bargany. Ardmillan is the only one of the Ayrshire houses where Queen Mary stayed which is today still standing and inhabited, though much altered. Here the equerry again entered *Neant* in his accounts, as he had done at Dunure and was to do again at Ardstinchar, the spacious and lofty castle of Thomas Kennedy of Bargany. This lay a short day's ride farther on, over the height of Bennan Head, with the steep rocky island of Ailsa Craig in full view most of the way.

Ardstinchar, like Dunure, stood high on a precipitous foundation, though not quite so near the sea, overlooking the mouth of the Water of Stinchar. Here the Queen stayed only one night, though her lodging was probably not inferior to

[1] *R.S.S.*, v, 1439.

what she had enjoyed at Dunure. The company may have been a shade less congenial, the welcome loyal rather than enthusiastic, more formal than friendly. Thomas Kennedy of Bargany was an elderly man and at this time possibly a sick one, for he died the following year;[1] the Queen's active host was probably his son and heir, another Thomas, who, though he won the reputation of being wise and courteous, as well as 'passing kynd',[2] was possibly a little stiff in his behaviour to the Queen. Though married for the past seven years to Lord Eglinton's sister, he did not, like Eglinton, hold by the old Church. On the contrary he was an ardent Reformer, and his signature, as 'Bargany younger', had been one of the twenty-seven appended to Knox's 'Book of Discipline' in January 1561.[3] Though he was willing to regard Lord Cassillis as 'his cheif',[4] his father had been at pains to make it quite clear that the family were not the Earl's vassals;[5] and both of them would receive the Queen as loyal subjects but in no sense as Cassillis's dependents.

Everywhere during the Queen's progress, the equerry had difficulties, when writing up his accounts, with the local names. Ayr he had rendered 'Era', and Dunure 'Duneura'; and Ardmillan, which he made into 'Ermelan', had almost defeated him. 'Arstinchel', however, was not a bad effort for Ardstinchar, better at least than 'Glainleux', which was his version of Glenluce, the abbey in Wigtownshire to which the Queen and her train rode on next day after dinner.

After riding down Glenapp, Queen Mary passed out of Ayrshire, which she was never to enter again. There is no contemporary report of what impression she made on those who there entertained her, heard her speak and laugh, or merely watched her ride past. But some evidence that she left them a lasting

---

[1] In June 1564 (Edinburgh Testaments, vii, ff. 374–6).
[2] *Historie of the Kennedyis*, p. 25.   [3] Knox, *ut cit.*, ii, p. 324.
[4] Acts and Decreets, xxxviii, ff. 182–4.
[5] Transumpt (22 March 1623) of instrument of 8 October 1557 in Bargany MSS (Ardstinchar writs).

and happy memory seems to lie in the striking number of Ayrshiremen who five years later rallied to her standard after she had escaped from Lochleven, and fought for her at the battle of Langside. The French ambassador, who 'rode to Hamilton to the Queen, and dealt between the parties for peace, but was not heard', told Sir James Melville, 'that he never did see so many men so suddenly convened';[1] and the number of Ayrshiremen among them, mustered from a county where the Queen's supporters might be thought to have been but a small minority, can be deduced from the long tale of those recorded as having forfeited lands and goods in punishment for their loyalty.[2] Most of them, however, gained remissions later on.

Bargany and his brother Hew Kennedy of Bennan fought for the Regent in that brief but decisive battle, as might have been expected; and Lord Sempill had turned against Queen Mary after Darnley's murder. But in the Queen's army were Lord Cassillis and his brother Thomas; Lord Eglinton, Lord Boyd with two of his sons and many of his name, and Sir Matthew Campbell of Loudoun, Sheriff of Ayr; also Hew Craufurd of Kilbirnie and his son William, David Barclay of Ladyland, John Boswell of Auchinleck, William Barclay of Perceton, William Stewart of Dunduff, John Schaw of Grimmet, George Nesbitt of Templeland, and the laird of Penkill's son, Mr. James Boyd of Trochraig. Another who suffered escheat with these was George Kennedy of Barclanachan, who with his wife had probably kissed the Queen's hand when she stayed at Dunure. More remarkable is the escheat of George Corrie of Kelwood; for although a neighbour and dependent of the Earl of Cassillis he himself was an avowed and consistent Reformer. Like young Bargany, he had subscribed the Book of Discipline; and he had also signed the Ayr Covenant of 1562 and the Bond of Association against Popery of 1567. Perhaps he was one who

[1] Sir James Melville, *Memoirs of his own Life,* ed. W. Mackay Mackenzie (Abbey Classics), p. 100.

[2] Register of the Privy Seal (unprinted), vols. xxxvii, xxxviii.

fell under the Queen's spell while she was at Dunure, and remembered it nearly five years afterwards.

Besides these, there are recorded the names of several men of humbler rank, like Nevin McCully in Aird, John Broun in Lane, and Gilbert Macilwraith in Trolorg, of whom nothing else is known but that they had made themselves culpably conspicuous at Langside. There must have been many others who managed to elude notice there or afterwards. It was not a slaughterous battle, for 'there were not many horsemen to pursue after them, and the Regent cried to save and not to kill; and Grange was never cruel, so that there were but few slain and taken'.[1] Besides, the two forces contained kinsmen, friends, and neighbours unwillingly arrayed against each other. The dead on both sides, according to one account, 'exceidit not the nomber of tua hundreth'.[2] Among the prisoners taken by the Regent's party were the Master of Cassillis, brother to the Earl, and the Sheriff, Sir Matthew Campbell. Eglinton hid himself in a house under straw until nightfall and then escaped.[3] He had been one of the first noblemen to rally to the Queen's standard after her escape from Lochleven, and was one of the last to yield to the inevitable and make his peace with the new government. Another faithful supporter was Cassillis, who for several years remained loyal to the Queen's hopeless cause and received many letters from her in her English prisons, signed 'Your guid freind, MARIE R.'

As she signed those letters, Queen Mary must often have thought of her early years in Scotland, and of a good horse, and a fresh salt wind, and the sun on the sea, and the fair castle of Dunure.

[1] Melville, *op. cit.*, p. 102.
[2] *Historie of King James the Sext*, p. 26.
[3] *Calendar of Scottish Papers*, ii, pp. 405, 407.

4

The Last Monks of Crossraguel

There is hardly a monastery in Scotland the ruins of which remain as entire as those of Crossraguel, a daughter house of the Cluniac abbey of Paisley, which was founded by Duncan, 1st Earl of Carrick, in the time of Alexander II. It lies in a sheltered hollow in the heart of Carrick, about a mile from Maybole, in a countryside that has changed little since the eighteenth century though a good deal since the Middle Ages when the new abbey was surrounded by extensive woods. The abbey church itself, the abbot's house, the cloister with its central well, the quarters of the brethren and the capacious storehouses testifying to the productivity of their wide lands, all survive almost complete although roofless; and the tall gate-house and the chapter-house and sacristy with their simple but handsome vaulted roofs are virtually whole.

I have known and loved Crossraguel since childhood, from even before the time when the Ministry of Works brought its ruins to their present secure and charming order, and it gives me pleasure to recall that their survival owes much to the care bestowed on them by more than one generation of my family while they owned the surrounding farms. Sir Adam Fergusson of Kilkerran, a cultivated and scholarly man, took care that his agricultural improvements should bring no harm to the abbey. 'This ruin,' it was written in 1794. 'is preserved with great care and attention, the tenants not being allowed to take down and use any stone from the abbey itself.'[1] Two genera-

---

[1] *Statistical Account of Scotland*, x, p. 494, note.

3. The castle of Dunure

4. Crossraguel Abbey, from the east.
Left, abbot's house; behind, gatehouse;
right, abbey church

tions later, in my great-grandfather's time, 'the ruins were thoroughly examined and made secure';[1] and my grandfather had the belfry gable repaired and pointed when 'the next severe gale would assuredly have thrown it down'.[2] It was an uncle of my mother's, too, who edited the publication of the abbey's muniments.[3]

It is not difficult, when walking among the ruins on a quiet summer day, listening to the bees murmuring among the wall-flowers and the ripple of the burn that once turned the Abbey's mill and supplied its buildings with water, to imagine the peaceful yet active life which its community of Cluniac monks once led. They were in every way a reputable little body. No scandals, even in the years immediately preceding the Refor-mation, attached to the brethren of Crossraguel; and indeed in 1515 they were formally exempted from a disciplinary visita-tion of all the other monasteries in Scotland ordered by the Pope, a fact which, as the abbey's historian remarks, speaks volumes for the good order in which their late abbots had maintained them. All the more therefore does the question suggest itself of what happened to them when the Reformation arrived and in the next few years the Crown stripped the monasteries of their great estates and bestowed them on lay-men.

It is seldom realized that in Scotland the religious commu-nities were much less harshly treated at the Reformation than in England. In Scotland there was no 'dissolution' of the monasteries. A few monks joined the clergy of the Reformed Church, such as William Kirkpatrick, a monk of Kilwinning who became the first post-Reformation minister of that parish, and John Sanderson, a monk of Glenluce who became 'reader' there, but none seems to have done so from the small group at Crossraguel. It was difficult for monks to change their way of

[1] *Crossraguel Charters*, ii, p. 89; cp. *New Statistical Account of Scotland*, v (Ayrshire), p. 782.

[2] *Crossraguel Charters*, ii, p. 112.

[3] Mr. F. C. Hunter Blair (1859–1940).

life, and most of them probably preferred to continue their quiet lives in the quarters to which they had been so long accustomed.[1] A few no doubt drifted away into secular employments, and some married. But for those who wished to remain where they were there was, as will be explained, at least no financial obstacle.

For the ruination or disappearance of many of our finest medieval churches the Reformers or the mobs they inflamed generally get the blame which properly belongs elsewhere: either to the Roman Church which had neglected their upkeep, the English who destroyed them in war, or subsequent heritors or local authorities who did not trouble or could not afford to maintain the buildings they had inherited. Actual violent destruction at the Reformation was mostly limited to the friaries. Many monasteries often suffered no damage at all, and their destruction was effected by some later generation for reasons quite other than religious. An example is the abbey of Deer of which Sir Robert Gordon of Straloch wrote, well on in the seventeenth century and recollecting the last years of the sixteenth, 'In my early youth I saw the church, the house, the monks' cells, the pleasant gardens and other things almost intact; but now the very stones have been taken away, and the plough is triumphant.'[2]

The Reformers of the West are recorded by Knox to have 'cast down' the friary of Failford and the abbeys of Kilwinning and Crossraguel.[3] But whatever was done at Failford, the abbey of Kilwinning served as the parish church for the next two centuries, and neglect and decay did not cause its great tower to fall till 1814. At Crossraguel there was probably no more than a formal 'purging' of the church itself, such as the destruction of most of the carved images and of those 'relics of

[1] See Gordon Donaldson, 'The Parish Clergy and the Reformation', in *The Innes Review*, x, pp. 13–14.

[2] *Macfarlane's Geographical Collections* (Scottish History Society), ii, p. 257.

[3] *History of the Reformation in Scotland*, ed. Dickinson, i, p. 364.

the choir' which had been formally handed over to the last abbot at his consecration in 1548.[1] All evidence suggests that the monastic buildings and the church fabric were left untouched—to this day part of the high altar in the church still stands, an almost unique survival. The last abbot, Quintin Kennedy, who died in 1564, was the uncle of the Earl of Cassillis who, as has already been told, remained a Roman Catholic, and Kennedy authority would have been enough to restrain any intruders from more than the minimum of 'casting down'. After Abbot Quintin's death the abbot's house, a high four-storeyed erection to the south-east, the newest of all the abbey buildings, became the residence of the successive 'commendators' to whom the abbey lands were granted; and in the monks' quarters the former brethren remained to live out their blameless days unmolested.

They were very few. The community at Crossraguel had probably seldom numbered more than a dozen, and at the time of the Reformation it was even smaller. There were only eight monks when Abbot Kennedy was installed, and only nine in 1560, or ten if the abbot himself is included—the same number as there had been as long ago as 1405.[2] Here are their names: Dean John Mure, the sub-prior, Dean Robert McEwen, Dean Michael Dewar, Dean John Mure younger, Dean Nevin McEwen, Dean Gilbert McBurne, Dean Adam Maxwell, Dean Gilbert Kennedy, and Dean John Bryce. It was the two youngest of these, Gilbert Kennedy and John Bryce, who survived into the following century.

The historian of Crossraguel, Mr. F. C. Hunter Blair, points to evidence among the abbey charters that there were monks still living in the abbey in 1592—'a later period, probably, than in any monastery in Scotland'.[3] But evidence which was unknown to him allows us to pursue their story for several years beyond even that date.

In their earliest zeal the Reformers had considered con-

[1] Protocol Book of Henry Prestoun, f. 6.
[2] *Crossraguel Charters*, i, pp. 40, 124.   [3] *Ibid.*, i, p. xlvii.

demning monks to live on charity. The first General Assembly of the reformed Church of Scotland had sweepingly ordained that all who had been 'in the ministrie of the Popes kirk' should 'live upon the almes of the Kirk with the number of poore'.[1] But a little later it was settled that the monks should be entitled as before to receive their 'portions' in provisions and sometimes cash also, to be paid to them by those who now enjoyed the revenues of the former monastic lands. The monks were also to be allowed to continue occupying their 'chambers' and their 'yards' or gardens in the monastery's precincts, and that the Crossraguel monks did so is proved by a reference to 'the pur men that hes the yardis' at 'the place of Corsragall' in 1589.[2]

This provision for the monks' maintenance does not seem to have rested on any Act of Parliament. But by 1569 the payment of 'monks' portions' could be described as 'the common practick of the realme', and it was upheld on divers occasions by both the Privy Council and the Court of Session. It is the continuance of this 'practick' that enables us to trace something of the history of the last monks of Crossraguel.

By 1569 there were only six monks left in the community, by 1575 only five, and it might well be thought that it must soon be quite extinguished. But in 1597 we find evidence of two monks still surviving, thirty-seven years after the Reformation.

The evidence is such as to make very clear the position and the rights of these two brethren. The 4th Earl of Cassillis, who had become the virtual owner of most of the former abbey lands, had undertaken to pay the surviving monks their 'portionis of victuall and silver usit and wont', and had apparently faithfully done so as long as he lived. At his death in 1576 he was succeeded by a minor, his son Gilbert, 5th Earl of Cassillis, afterwards one of the principal figures in the great Carrick vendetta between the families of Cassillis and Bargany, during whose minority the Cassillis estates were administered

[1] *Booke of the Universall Kirk*, i, p. 5.
[2] *Crossraguel Charters*, ii, p. 64.

58

by his uncle Sir Thomas Kennedy of Culzean, known during that time as the Tutor of Cassillis. In his twenties Cassillis spent some time in France. He was in Paris in April 1596,[1] in London, presumably on his way back to Scotland, on 1 May 1597,[2] and came home late in July of that year.[3] On 7 October he signed at Maybole, with his uncle Culzean as one of the witnesses, a bond promising to pay Dean Gilbert Kennedy and Dean John Bryce their portions as undertaken by the late Earl for the years 1595 and 1596 (when they must have lapsed) 'and all utheris yeiris and termes to cum during thair lyftymes'. The bond stated three reasons for this undertaking. The two monks were said to have done the grantor 'diverss gratitudis and guid deidis'; he was obliged as heir to his father; and he was also obliged as heritable bailie of the regality of Crossraguel 'to sie the convent payit and assurit of thair saidis portionis yeirly'.[4]

But Cassillis did not fulfil his bond, either because of his financial embarrassments, which were considerable in 1599, or because of his absorption in his quarrel with the laird of Bargany. In 1602 Dean John Bryce raised an action against him, complaining that he had never been paid his 'usit portioun' at all, not merely from 1597 but since 1576, the year of the late Earl's death. Cassillis behaved in rather a shabby manner in resisting this claim on the ground that it did not state precisely what the 'portioun usit and wont' had been, whether in money or victual, and if the latter what was the valuation of the victual. But Dean John had his facts and figures. His procurator produced evidence before the Court of Session of what the portion should have been—so much in meal, so much in 'beir' or barley, so much in cash—and the Court accepted it. They even allowed old Dean John's 'oath of verity' as to the precise amounts to be taken on commission in consideration of 'the greate aige and waikness of the said Deane Johne'. It appears that the old man had retired to Dumfries, for it was

---

[1] Register of Deeds, lxviii, ff. 2–3.   [2] *Ibid.*, lix, f. 394.
[3] *Historie of the Kennedyis*, p. 19.   [4] Register of Deeds, lxxiv, f. 363.

there that his oath was ordered to be taken. A month later, the certificate of his oath being produced before the Lords, they awarded him his whole claim, amounting to £722 6s. 8d., besides ordering Cassillis to pay him £10 of expenses. This very substantial sum must have assured the comfort of Dean John's last days.[1]

His colleague Dean Gilbert Kennedy was still alive as late as 1607, when we find record of his borrowing some money from a man in Maybole. Since his obligation describes him as 'Deane Gilbert Kennedy in Corsraguell', it is evident that he was still residing in the abbey.[2] The buildings were still sound enough for King James to have toyed in 1602 with the notion of restoring them as an official residence for his eldest son, Henry, Prince and Steward of Scotland, who was also Earl of Carrick, 'quhen he salhappin to resorte in thai pairtes'.[3] But this project was never pursued.

Since Dean Gilbert Kennedy had been a monk of Crossraguel under Abbot Quintin Kennedy before 1560, in 1607 he can hardly have been less than 70 years old, a very great age for those days. Twenty years before, in 1587, he had been censured by the General Assembly for 'profaning the Sacraments' by baptizing children 'in privit houses and fields';[4] for Parliament had in 1567 forbidden any but those 'admittit and havand power to that effect'—in other words, ministers of the Reformed Church—to administer baptism. But this incident, and his obligation of 1607, are almost the only events of his later life that we know.

He was not quite the last Ayrshire survivor of a religious order, for one of the Black Friars of Ayr, David Alison by name, was still living as late as 1617.[5] But in his own neighbourhood he must have been long remembered as a unique veteran of the old times. The incident of 1587 suggests that a

---

[1] Acts and Decreets, ccii, ff. 6–7, 297–8.
[2] Register of Deeds, cxlix, ff. 285–6.
[3] *Crossraguel Charters*, ii, p. 69.   [4] *Ibid.*, p. 58.
[5] *The Royal Burgh of Ayr*, ed. Dunlop, p. 99.

younger generation, bringing their children to Dean Gilbert for baptism, regarded him with respect and affection; and I fancy that he is anonymously commemorated in the names 'the Dean's mill' and 'the Dean's meadow' which survived on the maps of the farms around the abbey ruins for well over two centuries after his death.

If he was given to reminiscence in his old age, Dean Gilbert must have had a great fund of anecdote to draw upon. The older brethren at the time of his novitiate would have recalled for him the arrival of the dreadful news of Pinkie, from which so many friends and neighbours had not returned, and the first singing of dirges and requiem masses for them. They must have carefully described to him, too, the stately ritual, five months after the battle, with which Quintin Kennedy, the last abbot of Crossraguel, had been installed in office: an occasion that must have grown more and more splendid in retrospect as the drab years rolled over the decaying abbey in which there were no longer offices said nor anthems sung. They would have gone over, stage by stage, the reading of the mandate from the Bishop of Dunkeld, father abbot of the order of Cluny in Scotland, the presentation to the new abbot by the sub-prior of the abbey's relics and the keys of the whole convent, the high mass, the solemn procession conducting the abbot to his seat in the choir and thereafter to his carved central chair in the beautiful little square chapter-house; not forgetting the three notaries framing a legal record of the whole proceeding, and the congregation crowding church and cloister to watch it all, prominent among them the abbot's elder brother the Earl of Cassillis and a group of local lairds.[1]

Dean Gilbert would clearly remember Abbot Quintin Kennedy, the graduate of St. Andrews and Paris, aristocrat, scholar, and doughty champion of the old Church. He upheld the Scriptural warrant of the mass by preaching, pamphlet, and disputation, the latter maintained for three days in September 1562 in Maybole face to face with John Knox himself,

[1] Protocol Book of Henry Prestoun, f. 6.

and managed to preserve his abbey almost undamaged although the zealous Reformers from the north, formally rather than physically, 'cast down' a part of its church. It must have been largely through his influence that the Reformation made at first only slow headway in Carrick. In the first General Assembly in December 1560 it was a matter of complaint that the mass was still being celebrated in Crossraguel and in its dependent parish kirks of Maybole, Girvan, Kirkoswald, and Dailly, as well as in the houses of Lord Cassillis and the laird of Kirkmichael.[1] The abbey's wide lands, which the brethren had farmed so well and made so covetable a prize, Abbot Quintin prudently let to his powerful nephew the Earl of Cassillis, and he lived on in his tall, comfortable house in the south-east corner of the precinct, and died there in 1564.

Dean Gilbert could himself remember, in contrast to the ceremonies and the rejoicings with which Abbot Quintin had been welcomed, the chilly reception of Master Allan Stewart, the commendator to whom Queen Mary granted the abbey in 1565 as an obligement to his kinsman James Stewart of Cardonald, the Captain of her archer guard.[2] It had been a farcically unimpressive occasion, and surely an annoying disappointment for the pushing young courtier, of dubious descent from an illegitimate offshoot of the house of Lennox,[3] who had secured the post of 'furriour' or quartermaster of the newly raised archer guard[4] and from that stepping-stone at Court had at one stride grasped one of the richest monastic estates of the south-west. One December morning of 1565 he rode up to the abbey gate attended by a party of friends and servants and a notary public, bringing with him the royal

[1] *Booke of the Universall Kirk*, i, p. 5.
[2] *R.S.S.*, v, 2187; D. Hay Fleming, *Mary, Queen of Scots*, p. 271.
[3] He was probably an illegitimate son of Cardonald who was illegitimately descended from the 1st Earl of Lennox (*Scots Peerage*, v, p. 350), but his parentage is never more precisely stated than 'born of a noble family' (*Crossraguel Charters*, i, p. 144).
[4] *R.S.S.*, v, 1368.

letters under the Queen's Privy Seal and the letters of provision from the Archbishop of St. Andrews entitling him to take possession of the abbey and its lands. He wished no doubt to be received with all the deference and ceremony due to 'the Lord Commendator', as he styled himself. But if he expected to find the sub-prior and brethren waiting in a submissive group at the gate, a respectful welcome, a formal induction, the abbot's house prepared for his lodging, and a cup of mulled wine by a blazing fire after his cold morning ride, he found nothing of the kind. In fact he was not welcomed at all. Five years before the community had numbered nine brethren, apart from the lay-brothers. This winter morning the abbey buildings appeared to be deserted.

Exploring the abbey, however, the Commendator discovered at last one monk, Dean Michael Dewar, and obliged him to go through the ceremonies which should properly have been conducted by the sub-prior—showing him the entrance to the church, placing him in the abbot's stall, and reading the letters of induction. Dean Michael led him into the chapter-house, the refectory, and finally the abbot's house, and the Commendator, having thus inspected his new possession, left some of his servants in charge of it and departed. The notary's official record of the proceedings implies that they were the coldest and most unenthusiastic formalities.[1]

It is clear that Dean Gilbert and all the other brethren had deliberately absented themselves; and the solitary presence of Dean Michael Dewar, who had been in the abbey since 1547 at least and was probably the oldest of the community, implies something else. It was the rule of the Cluniac order that a novice seeking admission to it was received with a show of great reluctance. After being kept a long time waiting at the gate, he was at last admitted not as a welcome guest but as a stranger, and put under the tutelage of the oldest monks in the monastery to be instructed in the severest of their rules. Allan Stewart's chilling reception at Crossraguel suggested, and in

[1] *Crossraguel Charters*, i, pp. 146–9.

all probability was ironically planned to suggest, that the monks regarded him not as their superior but as a suppliant novice.

His abbacy did him little good, Dean Gilbert might have reflected. For one thing, the Queen granted Master George Buchanan, the scholar, poet and historian, a pension of £500 a year out of the abbey's resources. For another, only a few months after Stewart had received his grant she allowed the Earl of Cassillis to have a renewal, for 19 years, of the lease of the abbey lands which he had had from his late uncle Abbot Quintin, including the 'abbey place, housis, yardis and pertinentis', thus virtually annulling or superseding the grant to the Commendator. Cassillis was little disposed to respect the Commendator's rights and to see the abbey and its lands which two Kennedy abbots had ruled feed the fortunes of an upstart —even if the latter had married a sister of the Earl of Eglinton.[1] In August 1566 he began to make free with the abbey buildings, sending his chamberlain with several men to despoil 'the houss under the hey houss of the said place of Corsragwell and wallis thairof' of its rafters and flooring—'diverss geistis and treis of syndrie peices'.[2] He pressed the Commendator to give him a feu charter of the abbey lands. But Stewart was assiduously granting feus and tacks of the lands to various neighbours, his only interest in them being to turn them into cash for the benefit of himself and his kinsman Cardonald. In 1570 Cassillis kidnapped him, carried him off to Dunure, and by torturing him before a great fire enforced his signature to the desired charter. Even in those lawless days this behaviour provoked scandal, and Cassillis spent some time in ward in

[1] A sister of Lady Bargany (*Historie of the Kennedyis*, pp. 9–10), who was Lady Agnes Montgomerie. Her sister Lady Jean is stated to have been contracted in 1560 to a son of James Stewart of Cardonald, named (presumably in error) Matthew Stewart: no son of Cardonald's of that name is otherwise recorded. (*Memorials of the Montgomeries*, ii, p. 160.) Allan Stewart was certainly married for he left three 'lauchfull dochteris' (Edinburgh Testaments, xix, f. 186).

[2] Acts and Decreets, xl, f. 129.

Dumbarton castle. But he got his way. The Commendator parted with what was left of the lands in return for considerable sums of money, and by the time of his death in 1587 there was little left of the former Crossraguel possessions beyond the abbey buildings.

Even the 'yards' around the abbey which the surviving monks had continued to possess were alienated a few years later. In 1602 King James, who quite often did generous actions, especially when they cost him nothing, made a grant to a certain John Gray, the son of his former nurse Helen Little, of all the abbey gardens. The grant included 'the pasture within all the limits and bounds of the foresaid monastery's precincts, closes, and walls'—an indication of how thickly the grass was by now growing in the cloister and courtyards, and of how much of the outer boundary wall had fallen or been pulled down.[1]

Gray took sasine in one of the gardens ('for they all lie contiguously') on a September afternoon, and 'Dean Gilbert Kennedy, monk in Corsraguell', was one of the witnesses present. Perhaps he did not mind the loss of his garden much. He was too old to dig and weed it now.

Dean Gilbert would remember the year 1587 well. That was the year the Commendator died, a poor man for all his scheming, a mere tenant of the laird of Bargany, at his farm of Glendrissaig near Girvan.[2] The King conferred the vacant commendatorship, for what it was worth, on John Vaus younger of Barnbarroch. That was the year, too, of Dean Gilbert's own particular trouble when he was censured by the General Assembly. And it was the year of the Queen's execution in England, after which Lord Maxwell raised the standard of revolt in Dumfriesshire, hoping for support from the King of Spain, was besieged by King James's forces in Lochmaben castle, fled by sea to Ailsa Craig, and crossing to the Carrick coast came for refuge to Crossraguel. Denied admittance there,

[1] *R.M.S.*, vi, 1328; Secretary's Register of Sasines, Ayr, ii, ff. 29–30.
[2] Edinburgh Testaments, xix, f. 186.

he went to an inn in Maybole where he was flushed by his pursuers and finally captured in a wood near by.

But that was twenty years ago. And now they were all dead, these troublers of the peace of Crossraguel, except the present Earl of Cassillis, whom Dean John Bryce had worsted in the Court of Session, and the King who had gone off to enjoy his new English kingdom: all gone to their account—the blustering and blasphemous Knox, and the cruel Cassillis, and the grasping but luckless Commendator, and the Queen who had given him the abbey, and Cardonald, and Master George Buchanan. And Bargany, who had rescued the Commendator out of Dunure, was dead too, and his handsome young son whom the present Cassillis had slain on a dark wintry day as he rode home from Ayr, after years of feud and broil all over Carrick.

But old Dean Gilbert had outlived them all, and still had his familiar chamber and his 'portioun usit and wont', and his friends, and his leisurely walks out to Maybole, and his memories of good Abbot Quintin; even though the abbey's roofs were falling in, and its fish-ponds silting up, and John Gray's sheep were wandering among its buildings, and its mill and fields and meadows and woods and coal-heughs had passed to strangers.

5

Master Robert Cathart of Pinmore

One of the unrecognized masterpieces of Scottish vernacular literature is the *Historie of the Kennedyis*. The probable reason why it is so little known is that the only publication of it, edited by the learned and industrious Robert Pitcairn, was over 130 years ago, in a small impression which was never reprinted and has now become extremely rare. Another possible explanation is that the only manuscript of it, which is in the National Library of Scotland, breaks off in mid-paragraph at one of the most exciting moments in the story, so that as a work of literature the *Historie* is incomplete.

It is none the less an historical memoir of the highest value. The anonymous author, obviously himself a Carrick man and acquainted with many of the principal figures in his story, narrates the rise of the Kennedys in Ayrshire, the elevation of the Kennedys of Dunure to be first Lords Kennedy and later Earls of Cassillis, and then, in careful and vivid detail, the saga of their great feud with their kinsmen the Kennedys of Bargany. The surviving text fortunately includes the climax of the struggle—the battle at Brockloch, near Maybole, on 11 December 1601, in which the young laird of Bargany, Gilbert Kennedy, was mortally wounded; and its sequels of revenge, the murder of Sir Thomas Kennedy of Culzean and the burning of the house of Auchinsoull. There is no fuller account of any of the great family vendettas which bedevilled the Scotland of the late sixteenth century.

The *Historie* has naturally been used as a source-book by

James Paterson the historian of Ayrshire and by everyone
since his time who has written on the county's early history. It
has also been a quarry for novelists, notably S. R. Crockett for
The Grey Man. These borrowings are not surprising, for the
unknown author had a fascinating style. He writes in Scots,
the tongue which was in his day losing ground in literature but
was still generally used in legal documents and in all private
correspondence. He has a racy vocabulary and a pithy turn of
phrase contrasting strongly with the rambling periods of some
of his contemporaries. Generally his style is colloquial, not
quite that of a letter but rather of a man talking; yet on
occasions he rises to a studied eloquence, notably in his account
of the fight at Brockloch, which is a really magnificent battle-
piece, full of sharply observed details and vivid touches of
characterization.

As history particularly, the work is illuminating to those
who know the historical map of Carrick. The district has been
very little changed by modern industrial or housing develop-
ments, and even today the countryside is full of visible
memorials of the stories of the Kennedy feud. The old castles
of Bargany and Blairquhan, Culzean and Auchindrane, have
vanished, it is true, having all been rebuilt. Dunure and Craig-
neill, Baltersan and Thomastoun are only shells, and Ardstinchar a mere fragment, though each of them retains some
ghostly grandeur of its past. But the Earl of Cassillis's great
houses in Maybole and at Cassillis itself still stand inhabited
and scarcely altered, as does the Cathcarts' tower of Killochan;
and Ardmillan, as already mentioned, also survives. The buildings of Crossraguel Abbey are, though ruined and mostly
roofless, more complete than those of any other monastic
foundation in Scotland except Inchcolm. Beside the old moor-
land road from Maybole to Dailly, now used only by shepherds
and gamekeepers, you can still see, somewhat subsided into the
heather, the cairn marking the spot where Kennedy of Girvan-
mains ambushed and slew McAlexander of Drummochreen.
You may still stand on the high-arched bridge of Doon over

which young Bargany rode to his death three hundred and sixty years ago. And in the kirkyard of Ballantrae, below the steep craig on which his castle of Ardstinchar stood, is the aisle, somewhat weathered but today well preserved, containing the 'glorious tomb' which Bargany's widow made for him and in which her body was so soon afterwards laid beside his in September 1605.

Every page of the *Historie* shows that its author knew the topography of Carrick intimately. He is moreover an obvious partisan of the Bargany family. His affection for them appears several times. On the death of the old laird of Bargany, in the key year of 1597 when the final and fatal stage of the great feud begins, he gives a long and dignified eulogy of 'the nobillest man that ever was in that cuntry in his tyme'. On the death of the old Lady Bargany, too, he commemorates her as 'ane nobill womane . . . maist nobill in all hir effairis'. Young Bargany, the only person whose physical appearance he describes in detail, is obviously the hero of his whole story; and his widow, as I shall explain later, is treated with particular sympathy. On the other hand the author makes no secret of his loathing for the fifth Earl of Cassillis who brought about young Bargany's death, nor of his contempt for Bargany's pusillanimous kinsmen Bennan and Ardmillan. The whole story is seen through the eyes of a devoted, loyal, and even prejudiced Bargany supporter.

Who was he? His Bargany sympathies are the essential point to consider in speculating about his identity. Yet they have been underestimated in the only two theories of authorship which have yet been suggested. Pitcairn, editing the *Historie* for publication in 1830, gave reasons why he was 'at one time convinced' that the author was that sinuous politician John Mure of Auchindrane, Bargany's brother-in-law, because of his prominence in the narrative and the frequent reproduction of his exact words in conversation. Pitcairn does not say why he changed his opinion; and there is another explanation, as I shall show, for Auchindrane's prominence in the

story. Paterson, the county historian, disagreed, on the grounds
that Auchindrane could not have been a well enough educated
man to have written the *Historie*, and put forward a theory that
the author was Auchindrane's kinsman Master Robert Mure, the
schoolmaster of Ayr.[1] There is no evidence of any kind to support this fancy. But Paterson was on the right track. The
author of the *Historie* was undoubtedly an educated man; and
this narrows the field of inquiry to a very encouraging degree.

But there is no help to be got from the manuscript itself.
Examination of it makes quite clear that it is not the author's
original but a contemporary copy by some other hand. It is
rather strange that Pitcairn should have either failed to notice
this or not thought it worth mentioning. The copyist is plainly
not a Carrick man himself; for he makes several mistakes in
copying place-names,[2] leaves a few blank spaces where he has
altogether failed to read others, and dates the Earl of Cassillis's return from France, which was in 1597, as in 1565 (which
would be about three years before he was born). In many
places he has evidently been unable to read the manuscript
before him and has omitted words and even whole phrases,
leaving blanks never filled in. His own handwriting is very bad
and not easy to read. Pitcairn's transcript is far from perfect
and cannot have been collated, for he miscopies some words,
omits some others, often vital to the sense, and in one place
leaves out a whole line. In fact a new edition of the *Historie of
the Kennedyis* is much to be desired.

The history of the copy-manuscript is itself something of a
puzzle. There is no indication why the writing should break off
where it does—whether the original really stopped at that

---

[1] James Paterson, *History of the County of Ayr*, i, p. 105.

[2] I deduce that what the copyist really had before him, to take a few
instances, was Knokdaw for 'Kirkdall', Corsraguell for 'Caragall',
Kilhenzie for 'Schalzie' in one place and 'Keilmeny' in another, Grimet
for 'Grimak', and Cairltoun for 'Camiltoune'. He fares no better with
Galloway place-names, reading 'Feochtt' for Freuch, 'Barnebarony' for
Barnebaroch, 'Gairsland' for Gairthland, and 'Kirkcalffy' for Craigcaffy.

point or the copyist simply became tired of it. The writing, which is continuous and unparagraphed throughout, ends a little way down the verso of a page, and somewhat lower down there begins, in a different handwriting, an account of the state and government of Spain. Finally, to add to the mysteries, the two outer leaves enclosing the manuscript, on the back of one of which the last part of the description of Spain is written, are part of an English legal document in an English hand.

We come back therefore to the internal evidence of the manuscript. Its contents, including those parts which, as they do not concern the Kennedys, Pitcairn did not print, make it clear that the author was, to the best of his ability, a serious historian. His writing of the *Historie* was a deflection from the ambitious task on which he originally set out, and is really a very long parenthesis in it. The manuscript begins with the title 'The Descriptioun of Scotland with ane Cronickell off the Kingis thair Lyff and Descent', and opens with about thirty closely written pages of annals, beginning with the reign of the mythical King Gatheilus, husband of the Princess Scota, the supposed eponymous ancestress of the Scots. Then follow eight pages of more detailed history and another sixteen of annals of the author's own time brought down to 1611, which year is thus a *terminus a quo* by which to date the whole composition. The last episode described is the reorganization of the Privy Council after the Earl of Dunbar's death, which was on 20 January 1611.

We then get thirty-five pages of miscellaneous matter. There is a list of the sheriffdoms of Scotland, short lives of the Regents, a topographical description of Scotland similar to Buchanan's but not copied from him, and lastly an account of the origins of the principal Scottish families or 'names', the material for which the author states to have been taken from 'my copy quhilk I drew out of the blak buik of Skoun'. It was this section of the work which, so to speak, led the author astray. When he arrives at the name of Kennedy—to which he has already given significant attention in his brief account of

71

the country of Carrick—he embarks on his long diversion with this excuse: 'Seeing that thair is sum noittis for memory heirefter to follow off the name of Kennedy I thocht gude to conteyne heir thair beginning and how thay roiss to be gritt and sa furthe to this hour.'

Now the author has obviously read Buchanan and other historical writers. He mentions a 'Chronicle', otherwise unidentified. He has had access to the lost Black Book of Scone and copied out some of it. He knows what he calls 'Wallace buik'. A chance allusion among the family histories shows that he has read Chaucer. Further, the details he gives of the deaths of both young Bargany and his wife suggest that he has some pretensions to a knowledge of medicine.

It can be said without hesitation that there were extremely few men in Carrick in the early seventeenth century—indeed a mere handful—likely to be so well read; and in considering who was this anonymous author we can at once leave several of them out of consideration: the schoolmaster of Maybole, the various notaries, and the seven parish ministers, or rather the three—Mr. David Barclay at Dailly and later at Maybole, Mr. John Maccorn first at Maybole and later at Straiton, and Mr. John Cunynghame at Girvan—who were in their charges throughout the events described. For it is abundantly clear that the author was, if not a laird himself, a member of one of the principal landed families in Carrick, acquainted with the chief characters in his story and moving as an equal among them; and his view of his subject is certainly not that of a minister, nor of a notary.

I assume as a probability amounting to a certainty that our well-read author had studied at a university. By no means every man who matriculated in those days went on to take a degree. A recorded list of heritors and 'weill landit men' in the parish of Kirkoswald in 1607, which includes several prominent local lairds,[1] comprises twenty names not one of which has the prefix 'Mr.' indicating that its bearer was a Master of Arts,

[1] Register of Deeds, ccx, ff. 158–60.

which in legal documents is never omitted. A careful listing of Carrick lairds and their kinsmen living between 1595 and 1610 who were Masters of Arts collects only six names. But among those six there appears one man who could have been, and I venture to think was, the author of the *Historie of the Kennedyis*. The other five, at any rate, can be dismissed without hesitation.

I eliminate first Master Lambert Kennedy of Kirkmichael, who made singularly little mark on his times. He is nowhere mentioned in the records of Parliament or of the Privy Council, and though he occasionally figures in records and other documents as a witness he practically never appears as cautioner, executor, tutor, or arbitrator. He certainly took no part in public life in Carrick, and I deduce that he was either an invalid or a recluse.

Master Alexander Boyd, brother of the laird of Penkill, was a man of great learning, a traveller, and a poet—remembered today for one incomparable sonnet, 'Fra bank to bank, fra wood to wood I rin'. But he died in 1601, before half the events of the feud recorded in the *Historie* had taken place. Master John Fergusson of Kilkerran, on the other hand, did not graduate till 1610 and was only a boy during most of our period. Master John Chalmer of Sandifurd, a kinsman of the Boyds of Trochraig and Penkill, was undoubtedly a Cassillis adherent; and so was Master Christopher Cockburn, who was in the Earl of Cassillis's service and was among his party in the crucial battle in 1601.[1]

If the author is among these six, therefore, there is only one possible candidate: Master Robert Cathcart of Nether Pinmore, second son of John Cathcart of Carleton. Not much can be discovered about him. He appears a few times in the *Register of the Privy Council*, as a witness to various documents recorded in the Books of Council and Session, and in two or three testaments. But the contexts in which his name appears nearly all connect him with some of the leading figures in the

[1] *Privy Council Register*, vi, pp. 652, 760; *ibid.*, pp. 349, 694.

Historie of the Kennedyis; and I believe him to have been its author.

Let us again summarize what we have hitherto deduced about this author's position, personality, and attitude.

He was a gentleman, and well educated. He belonged to Carrick, and was especially familiar with the country around and between its two rivers, the Water of Girvan and the Water of Stinchar. He does not seem to have been himself a Kennedy; for though he often refers to the cadets of the family, calling them 'the Freindis'—that is, the kinsmen—he never says 'we'. Yet he was certainly intimate with the family of Kennedy of Bargany and knew their history well; for he gives what may be called the Bargany version of the roasting of Allan Stewart, commendator of Crossraguel, in the castle of Dunure and of his rescue thence by Bargany's men; he has detailed knowledge of old Bargany's dealings with the fourth Earl of Cassillis and with the lairds of Culzean and Auchindrane; he has witnessed the lordly housekeeping in the castle of Bargany in the old laird's time; and, as already mentioned, he loves and idealizes the young laird Gilbert who came so early to a tragic end.

Further, the author plainly has, for Gilbert's sake perhaps, a particular interest in his wife Jonet Stewart. Their marriage had been imposed on the family in 1597 by King James's order, which to a great baron like old Bargany, who might expect to choose his own alliances, was humiliating. It was, says the author, 'ane gritt wrak to his hous'—but he adds '—uther nor he gatt ane gude womane'. He pays close attention to young Lady Bargany's fortunes after her husband's murder. He describes her 'great anger' at the Earl of Cassillis's evading of all penalty for Bargany's death; her efforts to organize revenge for it; her fatal illness, the exact date and place of her death, which are recorded nowhere else, and her funeral. On all these points, wherever he can be checked, he is strikingly accurate, as indeed he is on a large number of others in the *Historie* once it reaches the period under his own

74

observation, a circumstance which makes one the more inclined to trust him where he is the sole witness.

Next, the author is, as Pitcairn noted, very intimate with the laird of Auchindrane, John Mure, and remarkably conversant with his movements and actions, and even his exact words. He is equally well informed, though Pitcairn did not observe it, about the laird of Carleton, John Cathcart, and his eldest son (Master Robert Cathcart's father and brother). The brother—John Cathcart younger of Carleton—was present at a vital conference of the Bargany faction in Ardstinchar castle, and also in the battle at Brockloch. He, just as much as Auchindrane, could have been the author's informant regarding both occasions, which are described in great detail.

Finally, though the author tells us nothing directly about himself, we can infer his principles in Church matters; for he calls Quintin Kennedy, the last abbot of Crossraguel, 'ane gude man, and ane that feiritt God efter the maner of his religione', and of old Bargany, who had been an active Reformer, he says that he 'was fra the beginning on the rycht syd of religioun'.

It does not seem that the *Historie* was meant for a wide audience. As I have already mentioned, its style is not literary but informal. It makes virtually no reference to national affairs—not even to King James's succession to the English Crown and his departure from Scotland. It is local history, indeed clan history, written entirely for readers who already know the scene, the outline, and the chief characters. My guess is that it was intended for the family charter-chest at Killochan, and that, but for the destruction of those archives about fifty years ago, the original might have been found there. But at any rate the author's attitude to his theme and his audience emphasize the certainty that he was a Carrick man and closely associated with the house of Bargany.

The career of Master Robert Cathcart fits strikingly well into this framework. He was born in all probability at Killochan, the home of his father John Cathcart of Carleton, whose wife was Helen Wallace. Killochan stands today just as it stood in Robert's youth (his parents rebuilt or enlarged it in 1586), unaltered but for the addition of an eighteenth-century wing, occupied, and admirably preserved. It lies near the Water of Girvan, about three miles from its mouth, little over a mile from the site of the old castle of Bargany and about an hour's ride from Maybole. Robert's parents were married in about 1563[1] and he was probably born in 1565, certainly not more than a year or so later. He was thus about 32 in the momentous year of 1597 when old Bargany died and the young Earl of Cassillis came home from France, and about 36 when young Gilbert Kennedy of Bargany met his end.

It must have been at Glasgow that he took his Master of Arts degree. The university's records are deficient for this period so that we do not know the date but may presume it to have been about 1582, the year in which Edinburgh University was founded. He married soon afterwards, at the age of about twenty.

Master Robert's wife was Agnes Kennedy, a widow with a young family, and she was perhaps a little older than himself, though not certainly: girls married very young in those days. Her first husband, who had died in February 1581, was John Eccles of Kildonan, and he left her with one daughter of her own, Agnes, and the guardianship of his other daughters by an earlier marriage and one bastard daughter. The Eccles and Cathcart families must have been on friendly terms, for the laird of Kildonan's will includes the sentence, 'Item he levis the young laird of Cairltoun his hagbut and tua pistolattis'.[2] This acquaintanceship easily accounts for Master Robert's having married Kildonan's widow Agnes Kennedy and settled down with her at Kildonan in the Stinchar valley, where we next hear of him in 1593. Three days before Christmas in that year Agnes died.

[1] They were already married by 24 September of that year (*R.M.S.*, iv, 1485).

[2] Edinburgh Testaments, xiv, ff. 210–11.

Master Robert's marriage had lasted only some eight years (presuming that he had married at about twenty). The terms of Agnes Kennedy's will suggest that it had been a happy one. She appointed her husband her sole executor, left him to divide her personal property among their children, and committed to him the tutorship of his step-daughter Agnes Eccles, 'faitherlie to governe hir as his awin'.[1] The testament mentions 'barnes' of hers and Robert's, but names only the eldest son John.

Within the next three years Master Robert bought the small estate of Nether Pinmore a little further up the Stinchar, and he is always described hereafter as either 'of Nether Pinmore' or 'of Pinmore'. He did not marry again. It may have been about this time that he formed a friendship with a young neighbour of the Cathcarts, Master Robert Boyd of Trochrig, who went to France in 1597 and there won celebrity as a philosopher and theologian, returning to Scotland in 1614 to become a famous Principal of Glasgow University; for on Master Robert's death Boyd mourned him as an old friend and as 'a man of great piety and experience in the way and life of God'.[2]

During the four crucial years of the Kennedy feud, from 1597 to 1601, Master Robert Cathcart is scarcely on record at all. His name is not mentioned in the *Historie* during that or any other period. But his father and elder brother appear in it several times, and, as I have already remarked, would have been first-hand sources for many of the principal events in the feud. Indeed the house of Killochan is admirably placed to have been a centre for the hearing and reporting of news of all Kennedy doings: close to Bargany, not far from Maybole to the north-east or the bridge of Girvan to the south-west, and forming one link in that chain of towers and manor-houses, nearly all belonging to Kennedys, which stretched all down the Girvan Water for more than a dozen miles.

[1] Edinburgh Testaments, xxvii, ff. 63–4.
[2] *Bannatyne Miscellany*, i, p. 288.

In the battle of 11 December 1601 when Bargany got his mortal wound, Master Robert's elder brother John commanded the main body of his followers, wearing, perhaps, the pistols he had inherited from the laird of Kildonan. It is in the weeks immediately following that tragedy that Master Robert appears on record again, and it is these appearances that seem to me significant.

'The Lady Barganie,' says the writer of the *Historie*, 'raid to Edinburgh and maid hir complent to the King and Queine, bot wes littill the better . . . for scho wes compellit to by the ward of hir sone, and to gif threttene thousand markis for the same.' That she did go to Edinburgh and that she did have to buy the wardship of her own son is perfectly true. The payment of the composition is recorded in the unprinted accounts of the Lord Treasurer, and the grant of the ward in the unprinted Register of the Privy Seal, dated 14 January 1602, just five months after Bargany's death. But the sum which the Lord Treasurer received, or at any rate the sum for which he accounted, was not 13,000 merks but 10,000.[1]

Yet Lady Bargany's total expenses on this unrewarding journey to Edinburgh may very well have included another 3,000 merks. There would be her travelling and lodging expenses, some legal fees to pay, and not improbably some *douceurs* necessary to enable her to reach Royalty's unsympathetic ear—even though she had been one of Queen Anne's maids of honour less than five years before. What is certain is that while she was in Edinburgh, six days after the grant of her wardship, she had to borrow the large sum of £816, equal to over 1,200 merks.[2] And there was one man well placed to know her financial difficulties at this very time— Master Robert Cathcart; for he was one of the witnesses to the bond for £816 which Lady Bargany signed on 20 January 1602. He was by no means the only person available for this purpose,

[1] Treasurer's Accounts, 1601–4, f. 18v; Register of the Privy Seal, vol. lxxii, *sub* 14 January 1602.

[2] Register of Deeds, lxxxvi, ff. 103–4.

for Fergus Kennedy of Knockdaw, who had been close behind
Bargany when he was wounded, Knockdaw's brother, and
another Kennedy laird, Hew of Clauchantoun, were all in
Edinburgh at this time.[1] It would seem that Lady Bargany
regarded Master Robert Cathcart as a closer friend than any of
these, and that he, a friend and neighbour of the Bargany
family but one who had not himself been active in the feud and
so was not being pursued by the vengeance of the Earl of
Cassillis or the Privy Council, had ridden to Edinburgh with
Bargany's widow to stand by her in her trouble.

The authorities took note of his sympathies a few months
later. In the interval, on 12 May 1602, Lord Cassillis's uncle,
Sir Thomas Kennedy of Culzean, had been murdered by Bargany's young brother, Thomas Kennedy of Drummurchie, and
his friend Walter Mure of Cloncaird, in revenge for Bargany's
death. The murderers were outlawed, and all the prominent
men of the Bargany faction were required by the Privy Council to find caution not to reset them—that is, not to give them
countenance or shelter. They almost all complied, for 'thair
wes ane gritt feir in all mennis hairttis'. One of those from
whom this guarantee was demanded was 'Mr. Robert Cathcart
of Penmoir'. He and Fergus Kennedy of Knockdaw were
mutual cautioners for each other, both their bonds being
signed at Killochan on 22 September.[2]

That was not the only indication in this year of 1602 of
where Master Robert's sympathies lay. On 28 January, only
seven weeks after the battle and while Lord Cassillis was in
Edinburgh justifying himself before the Privy Council,[3] Master
Robert had returned to Ayrshire and was at the house of
Auchindrane, in company with Cloncaird (the future assassin
of Sir Thomas Kennedy of Culzean) and Auchindrane himself;
for he and Cloncaird were two of the witnesses to a bond which
Auchindrane signed on that day.[4] This was another time when
Master Robert could have heard first-hand accounts of the

---

[1] Register of Deeds, cxxxii, ff. 160–1.   [2] *P.C.R.*, vi, p. 754.
[3] *Ibid.*, pp. 347–50.   [4] Register of Deeds, xcii, ff. 291–2.

battle, for both Cloncaird and Auchindrane had been prominent in it on Bargany's side. Cloncaird had killed Lord Cassillis's master of household, and Auchindrane had received a severe wound from the shot of a hackbut. It is noteworthy that the *Historie* gives the whole conversation between Bargany and Auchindrane when the latter tried to persuade the young man to turn back on his fatal journey, and describes how Auchindrane got his wound, his danger from it, and the relations in the next few weeks between him, Cloncaird, Drummurchie, and Lady Bargany, who, it says, was 'dealing with' Cloncaird and Drummurchie to concert plans for Culzean's murder. If Master Robert was not himself involved in these plots he was undoubtedly in very close contact with those who were. And the writer of the *Historie* certainly knew Cloncaird and had a liking for him. 'He was bayth stout and kynd,' he says; 'and giff that he had had dayis, wald have beine ane verry fyne man.'

There was another episode about this time of which Master Robert might have been an eyewitness. It also happened while Lord Cassillis was still in Edinburgh. For some time after the fight of 11 December 1601 Auchindrane was laid up, recovering from his wound; but he was evidently up and about again when Sir Thomas Kennedy of Culzean sought his help. Culzean was connected with Auchindrane since they were cousins by marriage and moreover Auchindrane's eldest son had married Culzean's daughter only a little over a year before.[1] Auchindrane himself was married to Bargany's sister. He therefore had a foot in both camps, and Culzean quite reasonably asked him to act as mediator between himself and Drummurchie and Cloncaird, who he had heard were plotting at Lady Bargany's instigation to murder him.

Auchindrane agreed to do his best, procured proposals from both sides for a kind of treaty of future neutrality in the feud, got Drummurchie and Cloncaird to come to his house, and then invited Culzean to dinner to meet them. When Culzean

---

[1] Register of Deeds, xxxiv, ff. 216–18.

arrived, Auchindrane talked to him in the hall, having persuaded the other two to wait upstairs 'in ane chalmer'. But
Culzean changed his mind, and said he could not enter into any
agreement without his chief's knowledge and consent. He took
his leave, and Auchindrane politely saw him home almost all
the way to Culzean.

Now this whole episode is reported in the *Historie* in great
detail, with the actual conversation of Auchindrane and his
guest, which gives a very strong impression of being more than
Auchindrane's own account, in fact the account of an eyewitness. In other words, it looks as if the writer of the *Historie*
was himself present. We know that Master Robert Cathcart
was on visiting terms with Auchindrane at just this time. We
know that on one occasion at just this time he was in Auchindrane's house in company with Cloncaird. He may therefore
very well have been the person who witnessed and recorded
this abortive attempt to limit the progress of the Carrick vendetta.

The Cassillis party, however, had the upper hand by this
time, and Master Robert's father, the laird of Carleton, 'maid
moyane', says the *Historie*, 'nocht to be trublitt nor to
trubill'. In the spring of 1603 occurred the last attempt of the
Bargany faction to avenge their lost chief. Drummurchie and
Cloncaird besieged Lord Cassillis's wife and brother with their
attendants in the house of Auchinsoull beside the Stinchar and
very nearly caught the man who had actually given Bargany
his death-wound, but he got away under cover of the smoke
from the burning house. This episode, most vividly described
in the *Historie*, took place only four miles up the Stinchar from
Master Robert's house of Pinmore, so that he could have had
ample opportunities of hearing all its details from his neighbours.

We find a record of him next in 1605, and again in close
association with the widowed Lady Bargany. Early in July
she was in Edinburgh. She was now a dying woman, suffering
from what was probably tuberculosis—called in those days a

F   81

hectic fever, or in the words of the *Historie* 'the eittik'. She was about to set out for London to consult the Queen's physician, Dr. Martin;[1] and before her departure she assigned the management of all her affairs to her brother Josias Stewart of Bonytoun. She was 'very far gevin over to his counsell', says the *Historie*, and there is evidence suggesting that his advice concerning the management of the Bargany estates was unbusinesslike.[2] The author of the *Historie* writes of it somewhat critically. Master Robert Cathcart was in a position to know something about it, for he was a witness to the five documents which Lady Bargany signed in Edinburgh on 6 July.[3] The same day she made her testament, bravely describing herself as 'haill in bodie and spreit (praisit be God)' and nominating her brother Josias her sole executor. To this document also Master Robert was a witness.[4] Then she set out for London, accompanied by Josias. The Queen's doctor could do nothing for her; 'quhairfoir', says the *Historie*, 'scho wald have beine att hame'. But she was never to see Ayrshire again. On the homeward road, at Stilton, sixty miles from London, she died on 16 August. Josias brought her body by the Sanquhar road to Ayr, and on 15 September[5] the bodies of her husband and herself were solemnly conveyed to Ballantrae and buried in the tomb Lady Bargany had prepared, beneath their stone-carved recumbent effigies. Three Earls, four Lords, and a thousand gentlemen on horseback formed the procession, which included a banner of revenge borne by Bargany's nephew, the son of Auchindrane, showing Bargany's portrait 'with all his woundis' and the motto which customarily went with such devices, 'Judge and revenge my cause, O Lord!' It was all done 'verry

[1] On whom see *Calendar of State Papers* (*Domestic*), 1603–10, pp. 205, 233.

[2] Register of Deeds, cvii, ff. 39–41, 129–30, etc.

[3] Register of Deeds, cx, ff. 134–8.

[4] Glasgow Testaments, xvii, ff. 114–16.

[5] The year 1605, left blank in the MS and Pitcairn's text, is confirmed by *Ayr Burgh Accounts* (Scottish History Society), p. 228.

honourabilly', as the *Historie* says, and no doubt very expensively too, helping to contribute to the ruin of the Bargany fortunes which followed in a few years.

These matters are described with a detail which, admittedly, many people in Carrick would have known; but the close and compassionate attention paid to the circumstances of young Lady Bargany's death suggests again that the writer was a near friend and probably companion of hers.

Little more is known of Master Robert Cathcart. He died in 1616, for it was in October of that year that his friend the Principal of Glasgow University recorded hearing the news. I was once inclined to doubt this as a false rumour, for five years later there is recorded an allusion to the marriage contract of 'Robert Cathcart of Neddir Pinmoir' and Auchindrane's daughter Elizabeth Mure,[1] and I had assumed that this indicated a late second marriage of Master Robert to a child of his old associate (who, with his eldest son, had been executed for murder in 1611). But as this Robert Cathcart is not designated 'Master' either in this reference or in his appearance as a witness in 1617,[2] I think he must have been one of Master Robert's sons. We know from Agnes Kennedy's testament that he had other children besides John the eldest. Anyhow, this marriage supplies one more fragment of evidence connecting Master Robert's family with that of Auchindrane.

Shadowy though his personality must remain—Robert Boyd's tribute to his piety is the only direct evidence of his character—it is, I think, striking that almost every surviving record of his life associates him with the families of Bargany and Auchindrane. That he did write the *Historie of the Kennedyis* cannot be proved; but it is certain that he could have done so, and that there was no one in Carrick at the time better qualified for the task.

[1] Ayr Sasines, ii, ff. 216–17.
[2] Kennedy of Bennan MSS (H.M. General Register House), 42.

6

A Ship of State

For the greater part of the sixteenth century the continuance of the Scottish crown in the house of Stewart hung on a single life. Queen Mary was the only surviving legitimate child of James V; James VI was Mary's only child; and he had no issue till he was in his twenty-eighth year.

It was therefore natural that both King and people should rejoice over the birth, on 19 February 1593–4, of the first child of James VI and his queen, Anne of Denmark. This was Henry, Prince and Steward of Scotland and Duke of Rothesay, who was created in 1610 Prince of Wales but did not live to succeed to the crowns of England and Scotland. It was natural, too, that the baptism of a royal heir-apparent should be made a State occasion. And it was characteristic of King James to make it a very extravagant one.

Preparations for it took six months. Foreign princes were invited to send special ambassadors to attend the ceremony, and the King scraped up as much money as he possibly could to entertain them in the most lavish and sumptuous manner that could be devised. He had already, even before his son's birth, induced the Three Estates to grant him £100,000 to meet 'the honnourable and maist necessair chargeis that mon be maid and sustenit throu this occasioun',[1] but that was not likely to suffice, especially as he resolved to rebuild the Chapel Royal in Stirling Castle before the christening service. There are many allusions in contemporary records to 'his Majestie

[1] *Acts of the Parliament of Scotland*, iv, pp. 40–2.

5. King James VI, about the time of his marriage

having ado with instant and reddy money for provision to be maid agane the baptisme of the Prince his Hienes darrest one'.[1]

The King felt that both royal and national prestige were involved, and was anxious that, disturbed though his kingdom was at the time, the distinguished visitors should be given an impression of peace and good order as well as of wealth and taste. He had summoned all his nobles to attend the baptism at Stirling on the appointed day, 25 August, and was much annoyed by the 'contemptuous disobedience' of the Earl Marischal who did not appear.[2] But at the last moment he recollected that large convocations of his lieges were seldom orderly and that, despite all the efforts he had made to compose or smother the many family feuds that bedevilled his reign, the armed followers of some of the nobles and barons were more than likely to come to blows in their masters' causes, and could not even be depended on not to molest the foreigners. Hurriedly he issued a warning on this subject. He himself must have drafted the proclamation which a messenger-at-arms read at the mercat cross of Stirling on 24 August, accompanied by 'thrie herauldis and thair coittis displayit and tua trumpetouris . . . commanding and chargeing all and sindrie our soverane Lordis leiges of quhat estait qualitie or degrie sa ever thai be of to set apairt thair particular feidis . . . and keip gude peace during the tyme of the baptisme as thai tender his Majesteis honour and estimatioun of thair native cuntrie'.[3] For its anxious and fussy injunctions that they should treat the ambassadors and their attendants 'freindlie and courteouslie', and have none among their followers but such as were 'discreit' and 'nawayis factious', is remarkably in King James's own customary style.[4]

But the ceremonies did not take place on the 25th. Queen Elizabeth of England's special envoy, the Earl of Cumberland,

---

[1] *Privy Council Register*, v, p. 160.
[2] Treasurer's Accounts (unprinted), 1593–5, f. 125.
[3] *Ibid.*   [4] *P.C.R.*, v, pp. 164–5.

had fallen ill, and the Earl of Sussex, appointed in his place, was delayed in his journey north by foul weather. The baptism was put off for his benefit more than once, to the annoyance of the other ambassadors—from Flanders, Denmark, Brunswick, and Mecklenburg—who were beginning to wonder whether their missions would not be so protracted as to compel them to embark for home in the season of autumn storms. But on the evening of the 28th the English envoy at last reached Stirling, though the French ambassador who was also anxiously expected never came at all; and the baptism took place on Friday, 30 August.

The ceremony itself, the tournaments that preceded it while the English ambassador was hurrying northwards, and the banquet that followed it, were all as magnificent as the King could have wished, and seem to have gone off as smoothly as anything at that period could have done. The invention, decoration, and general stage-managing of the ceremonies (apart from the actual baptismal service) were committed by the King to two of his courtiers, Patrick Leslie of Pitcairlie, commendator of Lindores, and Master William Fowler, the Queen's secretary, a scholar and poet whose sonnets, much admired by the King, are still worth reading.[1] Fowler was probably the author of a pamphlet, now very rare, which describes the whole occasion in great detail.[2] There are much shorter accounts by contemporary historians which Leslie and Fowler would not have thought did their ingenuity and trouble full justice.

Into details of the receptions and the tilting, the hangings of ' costlie tapestries ', the velvet and taffeta and cloth of gold, the

---

[1] *The Poems of William Fowler*, ed. Meikle (Scottish Text Society). Eight sonnets are reprinted in Miss M. M. Greg's *Scottish Poetry from Barbour to James VI* (1937).

[2] *A True Reportarie of the most Triumphant and Royal Accomplishment of the Baptisme of the . . . Prince of Scotland*, London, 1594. The text is reprinted, not very faithfully, in Nisbet's *A System of Heraldry*, 1816 ed., ii, pp. 151–60.

'propines' or christening presents from Queen Elizabeth and other sovereigns and potentates, the elaborate compliments paid and the commemorative knighthoods bestowed, I shall not enter. But there were some features of the banquet in the evening following the baptism so unusual and elaborate that they deserve full description, if only to show what the artists and craftsmen of a supposedly backward country could do when encouraged.

The banquet took place in the great hall of Stirling Castle which had been built by King James III. In the eighteenth century it was subjected to barbarous gutting and internal rebuilding to make a soldiers' barracks, and its fenestration has been greatly altered, but it is still externally a magnificent building. Inside, the hall was 125 feet long and $36\frac{1}{2}$ wide, 'roof'd at the top with Irish oak, like that of Westminster Hall at London'.[1] Here the King and Queen, the ambassadors, and many Scottish and foreign noblemen, gentlemen, and ladies assembled at eight o'clock in the evening. Five earls and three lords, preceded by the Lyon King of Arms and his brother heralds, with trumpets 'sounding melodiouslie before them', superintended the entry of 'the first service' of the banquet. With this actual hunger was satisfied before the entry of the second and third services, the purpose of which, as will be evident, was to delight the eye and ear as much as the palate.

The King, Queen, and ambassadors, on the dais at the southern or upper end of the hall between the two great oriel windows, sat at a table 'of three parts . . . that everie one might have a ful sight of the other'—in other words at a top table with two side tables at right angles to it. Down each side of the hall beyond was a long table at which the other guests sat, 'and betwixt everie noble man and gentil man stranger, was placed a ladie of honour, or gentil woman'. Thus the middle of the hall was empty and nothing obstructed the view down to its lower or northern end.

[1] John Macky, *A Journey through Scotland*, 1723, pp. 187–8.

So, 'having well refreshed themselves with the first service, which was very sumpteous', the company were ready for the two elaborate spectacles that followed.

To a 'melodious noise' of trumpets and hautboys, the second course or dessert, consisting of 'pattisserie, frutageis, and confections', made its appearance on a table borne upon a triumphal chariot twelve feet long and seven broad. Around the table stood 'six gallant dames', three in white satin and three in crimson, crowned or garlanded with feathers and jewels 'upon their loose haire'. Each carried an appropriate symbol and wore a motto to denote her identity: Ceres, Fecundity, Faith, Concord, Liberality, and Perseverance; and on arrival at the high table they delivered the dessert 'to the earles, lords, and barrons that were sewers', after which the chariot returned down the hall and passed from sight.

The chariot was moved 'by a secret convoy', which must mean a crew of men within it, presumably concealed by draperies. But the ostensible motive power was a blackamoor, 'verie richly attired', who was apparently drawing the chariot, to which he was harnessed by great chains of pure gold.

The blackamoor was however a last-minute substitute. The original design had been to have the chariot drawn by a lion, a real one, which the King kept at his palace of Holyroodhouse. Nothing could have been more fitting than such a personification of the chief figure in the royal arms, and Leslie and Fowler must have been sadly disappointed at having to do without it. The lion had been brought all the way from Edinburgh and new clothes had been supplied on the Lord Treasurer's order to the keeper and 'item to his boy' for the occasion, all at a total expense of just under £300. Imagination may toy with the thought of that journey: the lion restless and snarling as the wagon bearing his cage bumped along the road from Edinburgh, each relay of horses starting and shying at the sinister smell of the royal beast, the crowds running to stare at the extraordinary procession, and the anxiety of the keeper (and his boy) lest his Majesty's lion should come to harm. But all

88

we know is that the lion got to Stirling 'and thairfra bak agane'.[1]

Presumably the lion attended a rehearsal. 'But because his presence might have brought some feare to the neerest or that the sight of the lights and torches might have commoved his tamenes, it was thought meete that the Moore should supplie that rwme.' News of this change in the cast got about; and William Shakespeare, revising *A Midsummer Night's Dream* a few months later, felt confident of a laugh from a courtly audience at an allusion to it—'To bring in (God shield us!) a lion among ladies is a most dreadful thing. For there is not a more fearful wildfowl than your lion living; and we ought to look to't.'

But better was to follow than even a live lion. The third service consisted of sweetmeats—to be precise, of herrings, whitings, lobsters, crabs, and various shellfish all modelled in sugar; and these formed the cargo of an immense ship which appeared to a flourish of trumpets and must surely have aroused the banqueters to applause at the first sight of her.

This huge engine, though Fowler says that she 'entered' and 'retyred', cannot possibly have passed through the doors at the north end of the hall and must have been constructed inside it and concealed by screens under the trumpeters' gallery. Her length was 18 feet, her beam 8, and 'from her botome to her highest flagge' she stood 40 feet high,[2] the whole being mounted on a 'sea' 24 feet long 'with bredth convenient'. The pilot at her helm, dressed in cloth of gold, seemed to be in control of her course, for 'her motion was so artificiallie devised within her selfe, that non could perceive what brought her in.'

The men who heaved at the cranks inside the vessel must have been many and crowded, for this great vehicle was carrying thirty people or more, who must have been crammed, perched, or clinging all over her, like passengers on a Cairo tram-car; and the total weight must have been several tons.

[1] Treasurer's Accounts, *loc. cit.*

[2] The *True Reportarie* and Calderwood's *History of the Kirk of Scotland* each make a slip in the figures, the former giving the length as eight feet and the latter the height as four; but each fortunately corrects the other.

The visible crew of the ship numbered no less than twenty-four. There were the pilot, five mariners, 'apparrelled all in changeable Spanish taffataes', fourteen musicians in taffeta of the royal colours, red and gold, and 'Arion with his harpe', as well as three other mythological characters posed on the poop —Neptune with his trident, dressed in Indian cloth of silver and silk, Thetis with her mace, and Triton 'with his wilke trumpet'. As if this load were not enough, 'round about the ship were all the marine people': Parthenope, Ligeia, and Leucosia, with an unspecified number of 'syrenes' or rather mermaids—'above the middle as wemen and under as fishes'. These attendants were 'decored with the riches of the seas, as pearles, corals, shelles, and mettalls, very rare and excellent'. A further addition to the ship's enormous weight was her armament: thirty-six guns of brass, 'bravelie mounted'.

The whole of this nautical array was supposed to commemorate the King's gallant initiative in braving the perils of the North Sea three years before to fetch his bride from Norway, the symbolism being expressed by Latin mottoes painted on the white taffeta sails or carried by Neptune and his company. The royal application was further emphasized by the red and gold colours of the musicians' clothes, repeated in the draperies of the ship's tops and in all her flags and streamers. The two masts were painted red, the standing and running rigging was of red silk, the blocks of gold, and the anchors silver-gilt. The mainsail bore the arms of Scotland and Denmark, and the foresail the device of a ship's compass 'regarding the North Starre'.

A pause to allow all this magnificence to be taken in by the banqueters, and then, answering to the call of Triton's trumpet and the master's whistle, the mariners hoisted sail and the ship proceeded up the hall towards the dais. As she came she discharged her stern ordnance, the sudden explosion of which must have startled the ladies quite as much as the appearance of the lion could have done; and the musicians, with the sea-nymphs 'accommodating their gestures'—miming, no doubt, the motion of the waves—sang in harmony, *Unus eris nobis cantandus semper in orbe.*

Arrived before the high table, the ship rounded to and dropped anchor. Arion, 'sitting upon the galley nose, which resembled the form of a dolphin fish', played on his harp, and there followed music from the hautboys in five parts. Meanwhile Neptune was directing the unloading of the sugary cargo which he was presumed, as one who had before befriended and protected the King and Queen, to have brought out of his marine treasury 'to decore this festivall time withall'. The cargo had been contained in 'chrystalline glasse, gilt with gold and azure', and carried in the gorgeously painted stern galleries, from which it was now delivered to the sewers to set before the guests. While they admired and enjoyed it the musicians, who were evidently interchangeably singers and players, continued the concert which was the climax of the whole entertainment. The hautboys ceased and the whole ship's company raised their voices in a hymn of congratulation to the King, Queen and Prince in fourteen Latin hexameters. 'After which ensued a stil noise of recorders and flutes; and for the fourth, a general consort of the best instruments.'

After the last chord had died away, a voice—Neptune's, probably—announced, *Submissus adorat Oceanus.* Then, as 'all the banquet was done', grace was said, and the musicians sang the 128th Psalm harmonized in seven parts. Even in a psalm it was possible to continue flattering the King.

> *Blessed art thou that fearest God,*
> *And walkest in his way,*

they sang, 'with most delicate dulce voices'; and after promising that his wife should be like a fruitful vine and his children like olive plants, concluded:

> *Thou shalt thy children's children see*
> *To thy great joyes increase,*
> *And likewise grace on Israel,*
> *Prosperity and peace.*

91

The ship had yet to take her departure, and it was as stately as her arrival. Triton sounded his trumpet, the master's whistle echoed it, and the mariners weighed the silver-gilt anchors and made sail. Below the mermaid-laden sea the invisible hauling-team, who must by this time have been intolerably hot, bent once more to their cranks and levers, and the vessel moved down the hall 'with noise of howboyes and trumpets'. Just before she disappeared sounded her final salute. She 'discharged the rest of her ordinance, to the great admiration of the beholders'. The ladies no doubt screamed; a great cloud of smoke arose to mingle with that of the torches below the hammer-beam roof; and the show was over. King, Queen, and guests retired to another hall to enjoy yet another dessert, 'most rare, sumpteous, and princelie', and the company finally broke up at three o'clock in the morning.

For a fairy ship to vanish amid the cloud and thunder of her own artillery was wholly appropriate. It was in the tradition of courtly poets of Stewart times, and symbolized the awakening from a world of fantasy to the light of common day. Such a discharge ends Sir David Lindsay's *Dreme*. In the same way the ship in William Dunbar's poem *The Goldyn Targe* with her delightful crew of nymphs and goddesses, 'ane hundreth ladyes . . . als fresch as flouris', departs to the 'crak' of her guns 'till that the reke raise to the firmament'.

It seems strange that of all this remarkable entertainment the English ambassadors reported not a word in their official despatches. The reason may have been that nothing so elaborate had ever been seen in the English court and that they had no wish to arouse their royal mistress's envy. In any case they had more serious matters to report: that Queen Elizabeth's presents, 'a fair cupboard of silver overgilt, cunningly wrought, and some cups of massy gold',[1] had been safely delivered and gratefully received; that Sussex, as her special envoy, had been worthily welcomed (he had indeed been given the honour of carrying the infant prince into and out of the

---

[1] Sir James Melville, *Memoirs of his own Life*, p. 226.

Chapel Royal) and the resident ambassador, Mr. Robert Bowes, also accorded due honours; the tactless allusions in the baptismal sermon to King James's being heir to the English crown (a matter which Queen Elizabeth particularly disliked to be mentioned); and the unsatisfactory postponement of the King's measures against the Papist Earls in the north. Such was the matter of their letters. None the less it is recorded that 'the strangers mervelled greatlie at the shippe'.[1]

The cloud of her departure veils various mysteries. What exactly was the 'secret convoy' that gave her motion? And who was her designer? It may have been the King's Master of Works, William Schaw, who was in office from 1583 to 1602, or the 'maister wrycht', James Murray;[2] but the accounts of the Master of Works are not extant for this period, and those of the Lord Treasurer do not mention the ship. Some of the credit for her elaborate fitting out may belong to Andrew Melvill of Garvock, Sir James Melville's younger brother, a faithful servant of Queen Mary's till the day of her death, who was now one of the masters of the King's household and had had the responsibility of buying 'sic necessaris as is requisite for the decoratioun of the honnourable actioun of the baptisme'.[3] But there may have been some now nameless genius working under any of these officials who designed and directed the building of the ship. Of wrights, smiths, riggers, sempstresses, embroiderers, and painters there would have been no lack, for work had been going on up to the last moment to get the new Chapel finished, with 'the greatest number of artificers in the whole countrey convened there, of all craftes for that service, and his Majesteis owne person dailie overseer with large and liberall paiment',[4] Nearly £90 was 'delyverit to his Majesteis self to be gevin in drink silver amangis the warkmen'.[5]

---

[1] *Calendar of Scottish Papers*, xi, pp. 422–4, 431; David Calderwood, *History of the Kirk of Scotland*, v, p. 345.

[2] *Accounts of the Masters of Works*, i, pp. xxviii, xxxvi–vii.

[3] *P.C.R.*, v, p. 152.   [4] *True Reportarie*.

[5] Treasurer's Accounts, *loc. cit.*

The device of bringing in a banquet on some kind of fanciful carriage was not of course original, and this was not even the first time that it had been seen in Stirling. There had been a notable precedent at the banquet after the King's own baptism on 17 December 1566, when the principal course 'was brought through the great hall upon a machine or engine, marching as appeared alone, with musicians clothed like maids, singing and playing upon all sorts of instruments'. On that occasion the English ambassador's suite had been so foolish as to take offence at the accompanying masquers disguised as satyrs, whose long tails, ostentatiously wagged, they took for a studied insult, a reminder of the old medieval joke that all Englishmen had such appendages. Sir James Melville, that experienced diplomat, as he watched the blackamoor's chariot and Neptune's ship, must have recalled that embarrassing occasion of twenty-five years before, for it had been he who then 'excused the matter' to the affronted Englishmen who sat down huffily on the floor behind the tables 'that they might not see themselves derided, as they thought'.[1]

After the ship's one and only spectacular appearance, the artists and craftsmen who had worked on her must surely have felt some regret that she was to sail no more to the melodious noise of trumpets and hautboys, brave with flags and streamers, cheered on by Neptune and all his people of the sea. The guns would of course be taken out of her and the silken rigging, flags, and draperies put to other uses. But the ship herself was not broken up. She was removed from the great hall— presumably taken to pieces for the purpose and reassembled— and put into store. After all, the King might conceivably wish to see her sail again some day.

In about 1662 two English travellers, John Ray the naturalist and his friend Francis Willoughby, visited Stirling Castle.[2] They admired the great hall, 'longer, if not larger, than Trinity College Hall in Cambridge,' and in the Chapel Royal,

[1] Sir James Melville, *op. cit.*, pp. 84–5.
[2] See P. Hume Brown, *Early Travellers in Scotland*, p. 236.

long since deserted by the Kings of Scots who now reigned from London, they saw 'the ship in which they served up the meat into the hall when Prince Henry was baptized'.

There in the Chapel the ship remained for generations afterwards. Francis Grose the antiquary, Burns's 'chiel amang us taking notes', saw her there nearly 200 years after her one day of glory, and mentioned her in the second volume of his 'notes', published in 1791.[1] After describing the Chapel which King James had rebuilt for his son's christening, he adds: 'It is now employed as a store room; and here is preserved the hulk of a boat, in which the King caused the provisions to be drawn in, at this ceremony.'

The hulk probably did not survive much longer. Patrick Heron visited the castle in the autumn of 1792, and 'carpenters were busy', he wrote, 'converting the ancient state rooms into barracks, for the reception of soldiers—at the time when I was within the walls of the castle'.[2] He does not mention having seen the ship.

The Chapel Royal became an armoury, and later a quartermaster's store; and when MacGibbon and Ross published their first volume in 1887 they described it as 'cut up with modern partitions and floors so as to form stores' and the great hall likewise as 'divided into several floors . . . so as to convert it into modern barracks'.[3] But in recent years the partitions of the Chapel Royal have been removed and its mural paintings, of which faint traces had survived, restored by the Ministry of Works. Though the building is today not much more than a shell and is still used for secular purposes, something of its former dignity has been recovered. There is hope too that in a few years' time restoration will likewise begin on its neighbour the great hall, in which a N.A.A.F.I. shop now occupies the

[1] Francis Grose, *The Antiquities of Scotland*, ii, p. 238. Cp. Nimmo's *History of Stirlingshire*, 2nd ed., 1817, p. 279.

[2] *Observations made in a Journey through . . . Scotland in the Autumn of MDCCXCII*, 1793, ii, p. 441.

[3] *The Castellated and Domestic Architecture of Scotland*, i, pp. 470, 478.

approximate spot where the splendid ship rounded to before the King and the ambassadors on the dais.

Conceivably—just conceivably—the ship's remains still lie somewhere deep among the disused and bricked-up vaults below the great hall. But in all probability the hulk perished with the eighteenth century, thrown out with other rubbish or converted to firewood to warm chilly barrack-rooms.

7

The White Hind

The Earl of Mar was at the hunting. The sport was being provided by his old friend Sir Duncan Campbell of Glenorchy, a rich and powerful chieftain now approaching the last phase of a long and adventurous life. Sir Duncan's possessions of every kind were ample. He had had an enormous family, not all of it legitimate. He owned, as will appear later, several fine castles and towers; and he held wide lands stretching from east of Loch Tay to the shores of Loch Linnhe. These included several well-stocked deer-forests; and it was in the Forest of Corrichiba—Coiriche Ba, among the mountains forming the southern confines of the desolate Moor of Rannoch —that John, Earl of Mar, Lord Treasurer of Scotland, sat waiting for the red deer to be driven past him on a day in the early autumn of 1621.

The old Highland deer-hunt, of which Scott gives a description in *Waverley*, was an elaborate and complicated operation lasting several days and employing hundreds of men, or even thousands if some great man among the guests was to be impressed by the number of deer and of other ground game his host could provide. The great encirclement of the deer, or *timchioll*, would begin some days beforehand, the beaters surrounding a wide tract of mountainous country and gradually narrowing their circle until the hunt culminated in concentrating the deer which had been surrounded, and any other animals enclosed with them, near some chosen spot. Then a wild torrent of fleeing beasts would be directed past the place where the

G 97

gentry lay—or, in the usual phrase, 'sat'—in wait for them, as the Earl of Mar was sitting now. In some parts of the Highlands, notably Aberdeenshire and Perthshire, the driving of the deer was assisted by permanent fences of wood, or even of stone, extending for miles and gradually converging towards an enclosure. The Gaelic word for such an enclosure was *elerig*, which as *elrig* or *elrick* survives in place-names from the Moray Firth right down to the Solway. Another name for the same thing, *eileag*, is found in Ross-shire and Sutherland.[1]

If the drive went well, the climax was a vast slaughter of deer, some shot with bows and guns, many pulled down by the hounds which were let loose at the critical moment. Every guest expected to be allotted a place from which he could hope to 'get a fair loose for his dogs'.[2] These dogs were of an old Highland breed, 'of a very large size, strong, deep-chested, and covered with very long and rough hair',[3] which by the late eighteenth century was nearly extinct.

The end of such a hunt which Lord Mar had attended in the Braes of Mar three years before was thus described by a much impressed English visitor: 'Then all the valley on each side being waylaid with a hundred couple of strong Irish greyhounds, they are let loose as occasion serves upon the herd of deer, that with dogs, guns, arrows, dirks, and daggers, in the space of two hours fourscore fat deer were slain.'[4] But the slaughter was sometimes on a much greater scale. At a hunt near Dunkeld arranged for King James V in 1531, there were killed 'thirty score of harts and hinds with other small beasts as roe and roebucks, wolf and fox, and wild-cats'.[5] At another in 1655 in the Forest of Monnair, the Earl of Seaforth and the Tutor of Lovat 'got sight of six or seven hundred deer' and

---

[1] See an article by William J. Watson in the *Celtic Review* for November, 1913.

[2] *Highland Papers* (Scottish History Society), i, p. 205.

[3] Thomas Pennant, *A Tour in Scotland, 1769*, 2nd ed., iii, p. 159.

[4] P. Hume Brown, *Early Travellers in Scotland*, p. 122.

[5] R. Lindesay of Pitscottie, *The Historie . . . of Scotland*, i, p. 338.

had 'sport of hunting fitter for kings than country gentlemen'.[1] It was in the same year that Sir Ewen Cameron of Lochiel staged a hunt near the head of Loch Arkaig when the deer were so cunningly driven into a close circle 'that the gentlemen had the pleasure of killing them with broadswords'.[2] But sometimes the *timchioll* went wrong. At a hunt at which Queen Mary was present in 1564, the leader of a great herd of deer turned when attacked by the Queen's hound and broke back with most of the herd after him through the line of beaters, who had to throw themselves flat and let the deer pass over them. But, despite this accident, the final bag was said to have been '360 deer, with five wolves and some roes'.[3]

What sport Lord Mar had in Corrichiba in 1621 is not recorded. But the memorable incident of that day was not the number of deer killed. What he and his friends discussed afterwards was the singular appearance of one animal that escaped, a hind, which was pure white. True, the phenomenon was not unique. A white hind had been seen in the same forest in 1612 —in fact it had been poached, with many other deer, by one Ronald MacRonald of Gargavich and his men, to Sir Duncan Campbell's great annoyance. But Mar thought the fact worth reporting to King James VI, one of whose passions was hunting; and his report, made no doubt simply to divert his royal master with a curious tale, gave rise to a great deal of trouble for himself and others.

The year 1621 was a momentous one in Scotland and an anxious one for the Lord Treasurer. In the Parliament which assembled on 25 July, Mar had been a Lord of the Articles and assisted in the drafting of 114 Bills, one of them a Taxation Bill of serious import. On 4 August Parliament had been induced to ratify the Five Articles of Perth, measures which the King had long desired to impose on the Church of Scotland though much against the consciences of most of his Scottish

[1] *The Wardlaw MS* (Scottish History Society), p. 416.
[2] *Memoirs of Sir Ewen Cameron of Lochiel*, p. 143.
[3] Pennant, *op. cit.*, ii, p. 64.

subjects, and which, seventeen years later, in the reign of his less politic son, helped to produce the historic reaction of the National Covenant. Mar had ridden south on 5 August to meet the King at York and tell him that his wishes had been passed into law. It may have been soon after his return that he went to hunt in Argyll—a fairly energetic diversion for a man of sixty. He did not attend the occasional meetings of the Privy Council in August, September, or October, and only once in November, though in December he was hard at work again. Some time that autumn, presumably, he sent his news of the white hind to Court, for it was during the winter of 1621–2 that King James took it into his head to have the white hind of Corrichiba taken alive and sent to England. The scheme might appear fantastic, but the King perhaps recalled that a quarter of a century before it had proved perfectly feasible to send a consignment of twenty-eight live deer by sea from England to Leith and from there to the Royal forest at Falkland.[1]

The King's letters ordering this operation were dated from his manor of Theobalds, a little way north of London, on 13 January 1622, one directed to the Earl of Mar and one to Sir Duncan Campbell, from whose correspondence most of this story is taken.[2] But as early as 5 January the Duke of Lennox knew of the King's plan and wrote from Whitehall a letter of his own to Sir Duncan urging him to do his utmost to fulfil the Royal pleasure. He entrusted this letter to the man whom the King had designated for the mission, Mr. John Scandaver, a forester reputed to be particularly expert in the catching of wild deer.

Scandaver chose two assistants to accompany him. His

[1] Treasurer's Accounts (unprinted), 1595–7, f. 108.

[2] Two or three relevant letters are printed in *The Black Book of Taymouth*, but the more important are in the Breadalbane Collection in H.M. General Register House, Edinburgh. Some of the letters to Mar are among the Mar Collection, also now in the Register House, and have been printed by the Historical Manuscripts Commission. The spelling of the passages quoted here has been modernized.

party did not reach Edinburgh till about 6 February, when they presented the King's letter to the Earl of Mar at Holyroodhouse. Mar was somewhat disturbed both by the King's order that the white hind should be captured and by Scandaver's evident confidence of carrying it out. He had seen Corrichiba and would never have dreamed of suggesting such an attempt in such country. Moreover, the King was laying some of the responsibility for the execution of his orders on the shoulders of his Treasurer, who realized that he had in some degree brought it on himself by mentioning the white hind at all.

'We have sent this bearer our servant John Scandaver,' ran the Royal letter, 'for apprehending and transporting hither of that white hind whereof ye yourself gave us the first notice; and therefore have thought good by these presents to require you to cause provide, either at Edinburgh or any other town next to the place where he is to employ his travails, such things as he shall think requisite for taking or transporting the said hind, whether it be ships, carts, or other things. And because the country whither our said servant is to go is wild and waste, so as nothing is there to be had without acquaintance and special favour, it is requisite that ye write to Glenurchy (as we have done) to cause our said servant be furnished with company and all things necessary, as well for assisting him in his travails as for his own entertainment. And herein expecting your careful diligence, we bid you farewell.'

Mar's first thought was to warn Sir Duncan Campbell of Scandaver's imminent arrival; and learning that Sir Duncan's second son, Robert Campbell of Glenfalloch, was in Edinburgh, he wrote, on 8 February, a letter for Robert to take to his father, in which he hinted his doubts of the King's project. 'His Majesty has sent here a man who says he will take your white hind with some other deer—but for myself I believe in God always.' It was not prudent to commit to writing any questioning of the King's orders, even to a trusted friend, so the Treasurer expressed his doubts only verbally to Robert Campbell, adding to his letter, 'I remit all to the bearer'. He

101

asked Glenorchy to arrange to meet the Englishmen 'betwixt this and your house, for there is no remeid—he maun see himself'. Then he decided that there had better be no delay, and that Robert himself would be the best escort for the strangers. He added a postscript:

'I have resolved to send him directly with this bearer. Howsoever things go, I pray you let the honest man be as well treated as the country will afford. I remit all the rest of my mind to the bearer.'

Five days later the travellers reached Sir Duncan Campbell's castle of Balloch (since rebuilt and named Taymouth) at the foot of Loch Tay. Their route thither would have lain through Stirling, where Mar as hereditary keeper of the Royal castle there could assure the Englishmen's entertainment, and thence by Perth. From Perth to Balloch, Robert Campbell reckoned to be 'twenty-six miles if you go by Dunkeld and follow the river, but by the nearest way through Glen Almond it is only eighteen'.[1] Balloch was a strong place—strong enough to be chosen as a temporary refuge for the Regalia during the confusion that followed the battle of Dunbar in 1650—and magnificent and even luxurious as a dwelling. Sir Duncan in his time had waged war against the wild Macgregors and the 'broken men' who harried the estates of himself and his neighbours, and reminders of those rough campaigns were mingled with the comforts of his home. Swords, axes, hackbuts, armour, and steel bonnets hung in the principal rooms; but there were also arras, silk bed-curtains, glass, and fine linen; a dinner-service of massive silver fit to be borrowed nine years later by the Earl of Argyll to entertain King Charles I in Stirling; and a well-filled wine-cellar. Around the castle were the new-made grass-parks for the sake of which Sir Duncan had diverted the course of the River Tay at considerable cost, and flourishing young plantations of oak, fir, and birch.

[1] *Macfarlane's Geographical Collections* (Scottish History Society), ii, p. 538.

The arrival of the strangers under Robert's escort must have been something of a shock to Sir Duncan. From 'the principal auld man', as he later described Scandaver, he received one letter under the King's sign manual and another from the Duke of Lennox, who was one of the King's chief courtiers and also Mar's brother-in-law: the one requiring him to assist Scandaver in his enterprise 'and cause him to be furnished with all things necessary, as well for taking of the said hind as for his own entertainment', the other entreating him 'to cause assist the man towards the effecting of this purpose he is sent for, wherein you will do His Majesty a great pleasure'. From Robert he received Mar's letter and whatever Mar had confided to Robert's private ear. He realized that although what was required was practically impossible the Royal whim must be taken seriously, and that the three strangers who expected to be conducted into one of the wildest regions in Scotland in the height of winter on this fantastic quest would have to be taken there—and brought safely back again.

He wrote to Mar expressing his doubts of the whole business, and Mar, on 18 February, wrote back sympathetically. 'For the weather that has been here after their departure I know they have had great storm in their travelling. I am St. Thomas in this case, as ye are, till I have further news of the taking of your hind. I have delivered a transparent to the bearer which ye may let them have the use of to that errand, and all other help that ye can for their furtherance.'

'The 'transparent' was a telescope, as Mar's anxious postscript shows—'When they have done with the prospect-glass get it from them again'—but long before that rare piece of equipment reached Balloch the expedition was on its way westwards. Sir Duncan did not accompany it. 'By reason of my age and inability of body I could not travel myself without perilling of my life,' he explained, reasonably enough, since he was nearly seventy. The conducting of the travellers was entrusted to his son Robert, who was only forty-one and a vigorous walker.

103

The fortunes of Mr. Scandaver and his companions were narrated in two later letters from Sir Duncan Campbell, one to Lennox and one to Mar, and the course of their journeyings can be fairly certainly deduced. There was a possible route to the forest of Corrichiba up Glen Lyon and over a rough mountain pass at its head, but considering the time of year and the loneliness of that road a longer and easier one must have been followed, along which houses belonging to Sir Duncan would offer comfortable halts for food or sleep. At the western end of Loch Tay, some 16 miles from Balloch, he had built his castle of Finlarig, a handsome house 'decored inwardly with pavement and paintrie'; and twelve miles beyond that another castle, Lochdochart, set on a tiny islet in a loch. Thence by the kirk of Strathfillan the travellers would pass by Tyndrum up to the head of Glenorchy. Their destination was the hunting-seat which Sir Duncan had built on the edge of the Moor of Rannoch,[1] near the head of Loch Tulla—Achallader. The whole journey was nearly 50 miles, and they probably spent one night in the water-girt stronghold of Lochdochart.

Some of Mr. Scandaver's confidence in his ability to catch Highland deer must have ebbed away before he reached Achallader. On his journey from Perth to Balloch and up Loch Tay to Finlarig he had already seen mountains of impressive size; but as he rode north from Tyndrum he must have been awed if not appalled by the huge pyramid of Ben Douran ahead of him, towering more than 3,000 feet above his road. Those mountains to the north, his guides told him, formed the King's deer-forest of Mamlorn, of which Sir Duncan had been appointed hereditary forester five years before. Nothing could be more unlike the kind of forest familiar to Mr. Scandaver at Theobalds, Greenwich, Windsor, or Woodstock. Forest! A few stunted trees clung miserably to the lower spurs, but the huge stony ridges that swept upwards far above them were bare of any vegetation but the coarse grass that struggled for life

[1] *Statistical Account of Scotland*, viii, p. 347; *Black Book of Taymouth*, p. 35.

between the rocks. Snow lay thick on the summits which grey clouds sometimes hid altogether, and traced long irregular wrinkles down their seamed and rugged slopes. What a country to search for deer—indeed an individual deer!

As they advanced, the prospect grew more forbidding still. Ben Douran's peak was lost to view as the road wound close beneath it, but to the west, where the Orchy river poured loudly down its narrow valley, rose wave upon wave of still more appalling heights, cold, glittering, and precipitous, where surely nothing could live. Yet somewhere over there, they assured Mr. Scandaver, in a valley between those wild mountains just coming into view, was the haunt of the white hind he had come to seek.

They passed up the shore of Loch Tulla, beyond which, to the south-west, some dark clumps of pines broke the monotony of the landscape, and came at last to Achallader. It was nothing like so stately and comfortable a dwelling as Balloch or Finlarig; but after the rough road, the cutting breath of the February wind, and the repellent landscape, it was friendly enough. It had been burnt by the Macgregors eighteen years ago, but for the last ten years they had been completely dispersed and were no longer a menace. It stood close under the flank of another mountain, a small, snug tower, rectangular in plan, some 24 feet long by 20 wide, sturdily built of rough stone. From the hall which ran the length of its principal floor a narrow wheel-stair, corbelled out from the angle of the walls, led to the bedchambers overhead. The small windows that pierced its three-foot sides left the interior warm enough and commanded a wide view. A few hundred yards away a little river, the Water of Tulla, ran through flat, boggy ground to join the loch. Beyond the river rose low brown heights, and a few miles beyond them the great range of Stob Ghabhar and its attendant mountains which enclosed the forest of Corrichiba. Nearest of them heaved the broad whale-flank of Ben Toaig, on the lower slopes of which Robert Campbell, in his younger days, had overtaken and wiped out a band of Macgregors

105

in the course of his father's wars against that troublesome clan.

The foresters, urged by advance messages from Balloch, had been out on the hills for two or three days past, looking for the white hind. News was either waiting or arrived very soon that she 'with her company' had been marked down in Corriessan, close to the place where Lord Mar had seen her a few months before. So, on the morning of 22 February, the three Englishmen, guided by Robert Campbell and the foresters, started on the final stage of their quest. Having followed their presumable course in 1955 from Achallader to Corriessan at about the same season of the year and in somewhat similar weather, I venture with some confidence to reconstruct their experiences, reading between the lines of Sir Duncan's letters and allowing for the Englishmen's unfamiliarity with Highland hills.

To begin with, it must have been broken to Mr. Scandaver that to ride across the Moor of Rannoch was an impossibility: he would have to walk. Perhaps Robert Campbell advised him to adopt the Highland dress which he wore himself; perhaps, on hearing of the bogs, pools, and burns which he would have to cross, he insisted on sticking to his thigh-long riding-boots. From the start he may have guessed, if he could not altogether imagine, the ordeal that was before him.

The weather, as reported later to Sir Duncan, was 'vehement'. While fording the Water of Tulla and climbing the rough slopes beyond it, the travellers would be in comparative shelter; but before long they would find themselves on the open moor, trudging westwards over its high ridges nearly in the teeth of a fierce wind rushing up Glen Orchy and pouring over the snowy heights of Stob Ghabhar, perhaps laden with sleet or chilly rain.

'Pray,' wrote the author of a Victorian guide-book some 250 years later—'Pray imagine the Moor of Rannoch, for who can describe it?' An eighteenth-century traveller, Thomas Pennant, made a weak attempt to do so in nine words—'Truly melancholy, almost one continued scene of dusky moors'.[1] It would be interesting to know how deeply Mr. Scandaver, when recounting his experiences afterwards, drew on the rich resources of Jacobean English. If he was a playgoer when in London, he may have recalled a line of Shakespeare's concerning

> *Deserts idle,*
> *Rough quarries, rocks, and hills whose heads touch heaven,*

but not even Shakespeare had attempted to depict in words such a wilderness as that in which Scandaver found himself half an hour after quitting Achallader.

The moor was far from flat. It heaved itself up and down into ridges and hillocks, some of them actual hills several hundred feet high, and in the hollows between them little burns meandered circuitously towards Loch Tulla, among dark sinister pools. The ground oozed water at the pressure of a foot even where it looked solid, and though the pools seemed shallow there was black mud under them of unknown depth. Where they could not avoid crossing the low places they had to pick there way with care. The most practicable route across the moor was by the ridges between the head-waters of the burns, but to keep this firmer ground necessitated many detours. It was fatiguing walking, and the strangers envied the nimble, kilted Highlanders—the 'Redshanks' as they called them—whose muscular legs seemed to know instinctively where to tread and wasted no step.

The moor was clear of snow except in some hollows. It was clothed with a long, coarse grass, bleached and pale, with a few grey boulders and occasional patches of brown and withered heather. The wind, plucking violently at cloaks and plaids, howled so that they had to converse in shouts. Not that there was much to talk about. An occasional grouse raised its hoarse rattling cry but there was no other life around them; and the monotonous scene hardly varied. Only, as they slowly

[1] Pennant, *op. cit.*, iii, p. 233.

advanced, the huge, bleak mountains ahead loomed larger. They began to resemble a row of gigantic teeth, the lower jaw of a mouth yawning so vastly that the upper one was invisible in the clouds. And between two of those great triangular fangs, Mr. Scandaver learned, led the way to his quarry.

They could not make for Corriessan directly, for a small loch had to be avoided. Rounding its southern end, they turned north under Ben Toaig and approached the Water of Ba, the recognized boundary of the Forest of Corrichiba. It was a broad, swift stream which drained the great amphitheatre of Corrichiba itself, hurrying the waters of a score of snow-fed burns far out into the moor to form a chain of lochs of their own, ending in Loch Ba on whose remote islets the heron and the osprey nested. Ben Toaig sheltered the party from the pitiless wind for a time, but as they began to cross the open floor of Corrichiba it swept yelling down on them again, more keen than ever from the icy heights it crossed. The wind as much as the rough walking must have contributed to Mr. Scandaver's now evident fatigue.

After some three hours of this toilsome march from Achallader they forded the Water of Ba, crossed the boggy flats beyond, and began to ascend the north side of the valley. The prospect ahead was menacing. To their right rose a round-topped hill, its rock-strewn slopes sweeping upward into a rampart of short cliffs against the sky. To their left, a huge spur ran down towards them, knife-edged, covered with snow except where perpendicular rock-faces projected through it. Between, a laborious climb led up into the mouth of another, narrowing valley, streaming with little burns, which curved steeply leftwards out of sight against a snow-streaked ridge that overtopped both the round hill and the sharp spur. Up there, Robert Campbell explained, shouting against the wind, up that hillside strewn with rocks and pouring with water, lay their route. That was Corriessan—Coire an Easain, the hollow of the waterfalls.

Mr. Scandaver struggled forward to the throat of the corrie, to the place where, he was told, my Lord of Mar had 'sat at the hunting'. But the slope grew steeper and his breath and his heart both failed him as he stumbled among the rocks. To his right and left the waters poured; the Ba roared behind him and the bitter wind whistled overhead. He looked round him at the strange shaggy men chattering their incomprehensible language, at the high, cruel peaks, at the awful valley opening above him, a staircase of rock-ribbed snow stretching away round and out of sight up towards the cold sky. It was too much: 'the weather', as Sir Duncan wrote afterwards, 'was so vehement and the way so evil and rough'. He sat down and 'alleged he could go no further neither on horse nor foot'.

Long before this abysmal moment Mr. Scandaver must have abandoned all hope of catching the white hind. Whatever was the 'art' in which he was reputedly skilled, whatever combination of beaters, hurdles, stakes and nets he was used to employing in Windsor Forest, he must hours ago have realized was utterly impracticable in the vast and savage wilderness to which his Royal master had sent him. But he was to learn that his quarry was at least no myth. Sir Duncan's letter to Lord Mar describes the climax, or rather the anti-climax, of the quest.

'The other twa Englishmen that were with him passed forward with Robert and the foresters a mile up the hill, and there they saw the white hind with her company to the number of five or six score of deer, and sae they came back both tired and wearied. The twa Englishmen that saw the hind declares that she was as white as ane white sheep, and might easily ken her afar off by [i.e. apart from] the rest of the deer.'

There in the mouth of Corriessan, just 333 years after John Scandaver's admission of defeat, I too looked up the hill and saw a company of deer, not five or six score but at least some fifty. Is was satisfying to know that after more than three centuries the deer of Corrichiba still kept the same winter haunts as their ancestors. But though I watched them as they moved in a slow file up the corrie, I could detect no beast among them 'as white as ane white sheep'.

How they got Mr. Scandaver back to Achallader is not told. He must have been nearly exhausted, and his English companions, 'tired and wearied', little better. But it is evident that their hosts did all they could do to restore them. Every compliment that Highland courtesy could suggest would be heaped on them for their enterprise and endurance, and their success in actually sighting the fabulous hind enlarged upon as hardly second to her capture. The little hall of Achallader would be cheerfully warmed and lit by a huge fire of old fir-roots from the moor. There would be a plentiful supper, and perhaps a harper improvising ballads in the strangers' honour, with Robert Campbell considerately translating. 'As to their entertainment,' wrote Sir Duncan, 'truly they got the best that could be gotten this time of year in the country, for they wanted not wine and aquavitae—as I doubt not but they will declare themselves.' By the time the Highlanders rolled Mr. Scandaver into bed, he was, it may be hoped, in a roseate glow of satisfaction at having at least done the best he could to carry out the King's impossible orders, mingled with a deep thankfulness at having escaped alive out of those frightful mountains and that treacherous moor.

They returned to Balloch and held a long consultation with Sir Duncan Campbell. Having seen the kind of country where the white hind lived, the chastened experts were satisfied of the impossibility of catching her there or carrying her out of it alive—'whilk', commented Sir Duncan, 'I believe to be true'. They considered an alternative scheme: to construct a 'parok' or large enclosure 'in some wood where there is deer' in a locality to which carts and horses could be brought, and then to drive the white hind and her company to the place and induce her to join the deer already enclosed. Glenfinlass, since it was only a few miles from Stirling and salt water, would be the likeliest place for such a project, Sir Duncan thought, but he doubted if even the low-country deer could be so entrapped,

let alone the mountain deer, and suggested that the Englishmen had better make the experiment on the Glenfinlass deer
first.

The forester of Corrichiba was consulted. His opinion was
that 'with a right south wind the hind and part of her company might be driven out of Corrichiba' by twenty-four or
thirty men; but that if it was proposed to drive them for many
miles down through the glens, stopping every possible outlet of
escape on the way, 'two or three thousand men is the least that
can be put to that'. In any case, 'he thinks that she shall never
be taken quick to London, but that either in the chasing,
taking, or carrying she will die; and so', concluded Sir Duncan,
'I am of that opinion'. He wrote a similar but much briefer
report to the Duke of Lennox, and bade farewell to his English
guests, who rode back to Edinburgh.

The Earl of Mar replied about the 1st of March:

'Cousin,—I have received your letter and have spoken both
with this bearer and with the English men. I have sent your
letters and also my own this same day away by packet. What
will be His Majesty's resolution God knows. We shall ever be
ready to obey all possible commands. However the matter go,
I am glad they have seen her so as I will not be counted a liar.
Thus remitting all farther to the bearer, I rest

Your loving cousin

MAR.'

Scandaver made his report by the same 'packet' as Lord
Mar, and a reply soon arrived, dated from Theobalds on
9 March, from Sir Patrick Murray, a Gentleman of the Privy
Chamber who was also Keeper of the Park of Theobalds and a
favourite courtier of the King's (he became Earl of Tullibardine a few years later). From the cheerful opening of Sir Patrick's letter Sir Duncan learned that the King was not greatly
displeased at the failure of the expedition to capture the white
hind.

'Noble Chief,' began Sir Patrick, 'I have received from the

111

Earl of Mar a packet of letters concerning the taking of this
troublesome white hind of yours, and has delivered and read
them to His Majesty, he being not well of a pain in his legs—I
dare not say the gout. His Majesty is well pleased with you for
the care you have had to further His Majesty's desire in all
things concerning this business of taking this deer.' Mar's and
Scandaver's letters, he went on to explain, had clearly convinced the King of the difficulty of executing his wishes. He
had accordingly ordered that the hind should be left alone for
the present, especially since she might be in calf, and that the
strictest injunctions should be sent to 'all those that borders or
marches with Corrachaba that none presume to stir her, under
His Majesty's highest displeasure.' He would think of some
other plan against the following year. Meanwhile, Scandaver
was to try what he could 'do by his art' in the Forest of
Glenartney by way of experiment, and the Earl of Perth had
been instructed accordingly.

There is no evidence that Scandaver and his companions had
any success in Glenartney, but they must have made some
attempt since they apparently did not return to London before
July. On the 24th of that month the King, having heard what
Scandaver had to tell, sent Sir Duncan Campbell a letter of
warm commendation. Scandaver had evidently spoken in
glowing terms of the willing assistance and above all of the
unbounded hospitality which he had received in Perthshire,
and such reports were certain to please the King, who was
always anxious to promote good feeling between his Scottish
and English subjects. He expressed his appreciation to
Glenorchy not only for his 'earnest endeavours' but for his
'special care and good entertainment of Scandaver himself,
which as it hath given him occasion to speak of that our kingdom in general and of you in particular as of people dutifully
devoted to their prince and well affected to strangers, so we
give you most hearty thanks for the same'.

I can find no record of whether King James did ever think of
any other plan for catching the white hind. None seems to have

been attempted before he died, less than three years later. But Mr. Scandaver plainly derived much professional benefit from his Highland adventure. His career can be traced through the State Papers for the rest of King James's reign, though King Charles I, who was not so passionately devoted to the chase as his father, seems not to have retained him in employment. He specialized in the catching and transporting of deer to or from Theobalds, Windsor, Woodstock, Newhall Park in Essex, and Burghley-on-the Hill in Rutland. He caught his deer by making paddocks into which to drive them, and received large grants from the English Treasurer for the expenses of doing so.

No doubt he often bored his subordinates with his Scottish reminiscences, especially if they raised any objection to some proposed operations on grounds of the difficulty of the country or the rigour of the weather. But it does not appear that he ever again ventured further north than Yorkshire.

8

The End of Barbara Fea

Of few women can it be said that their principal characteristic is tenacity. But that is the only possible epitaph of Barbara Fea. The wrong she considered herself to have suffered early in life fired her to a passionate quest for justice, if not for revenge, which she pursued to the end of her days with a relentless purpose, from her native Orkney to Edinburgh and London and back again. Death itself hardly stopped her.

Her determination reaped some success. She almost ruined the family of her opponents; and she kept alive one of the longest lawsuits in Scottish history. It lasted for fifty-nine years, affected the lives of four generations, and was not concluded till Barbara herself had lain for nearly thirty years in her grave. What it cost, from first to last, is beyond computation.

I first came on Barbara Fea's story shortly before the Second World War. It was not till sixteen years later that I discovered the end of it. But so powerfully does Barbara's personality burn through the tedious legal papers in which the tale is buried, that it was as impossible for me to have forgotten it as it was for those who first found and were fascinated by it.[1]

[1] Mr. C. E. S. Walls, in 'An Eighteenth Century Orkney Litigation' (*Proceedings of the Orkney Antiquarian Society*, vol. x, 1932), has summarized the main story, and Dr. Hugh Marwick, O.B.E., in *Merchant Lairds of Long Ago*, 1936, has printed the Traill family correspondence. I gratefully acknowledge these as my main sources for the following narrative.

Barbara was born, towards the end of King Charles II's reign, in Stronsay, one of the most fertile of the northern group of the Orkneys—a disjointed sort of island, all bays and peninsulas, with a coast-line of over twenty-five miles, though no part of it is more than a mile from the sea. Barbara was the daughter of a Stronsay laird, Patrick Fea of Whitehall, in the north of the island. She had at least two sisters, Elizabeth, married in 1697 to the minister of Kirkwall, and Katherine, known as Kitt; and three brothers. The eldest brother, James, was in 1697 master of a Kirkwall ship, the *Elephant*, belonging to John Traill of Elsness, a laird in the neighbouring isle of Sanday. It was John Traill's elder son Patrick who was at once the instrument of Barbara's injury and the chief victim of her wrath.

The Traills and the Feas were cousins, and both families, like those of many Orkney lairds of those days, combined farm-ing with overseas trade. Thus Patrick Traill and Barbara Fea might well have become acquainted even if Patrick's father had not sent him over to Stronsay to manage his farm or Housby which lay, facing south-east, on the coast near the south point of that island. In the course of the year 1700, when Patrick was about twenty-one, their acquaintance ripened, and early in 1701 it grew intimate. Barbara's claim later was that Patrick seduced her under promise of marriage. Every-thing in their subsequent story suggests that Barbara was the pursuer and Patrick the pursued. In comparison with her, as Dr. Marwick says, Patrick 'was like a silly lamb caged in with a tigress'.

What is certain is that by the approach of Christmas, 1701, Barbara was expecting a child and Patrick had fled from Stronsay and was writing from Kirkwall to his brother David imploring him to look after Barbara and also to 'interseid with my father and mother for a pardone'.

In other matters Patrick did not lack enterprise or courage, but in his dealings with Barbara he generally appears pusillani-mous. Nothing is known of their brief idyll in Stronsay beyond two remarks in his letter to David—'Do not walk in my foot steaps for if you do I ashure [you] you will repent' and 'What I did I swear that I was obleedged to do or otherways I hade been afrunted'. He did write to Barbara, 'God willing you shall see me shortly with the olive branch in my mouth', but his courage failed him. Leaving all his responsibilities to David, a practical and cool-headed young man, he fled from Orkney, and did not set foot in his native island again for nearly eighteen years.

Barbara's child, a daughter named Jean, was adopted and brought up by the Traills, but they were utterly opposed to Patrick's marrying Barbara. She may already have displayed that fiendish temper of which she gave so much evidence in later life. But certainly she had good reason for resentment as, leaving her baby at Elsness, she set off alone in pursuit of the man whom she was determined to make her husband. The appalling determination of her character is reflected in the references to her in the Traill family correspondence. She is never mentioned by name. When she is not simply 'B.F.' she is styled 'the woman', 'that wicked wretch of a woman', 'the hellish imp', 'that venomous serpent', 'that vagabond' or 'vagabond strumpet'—epithets which, however unjust, are a testimony to the positive terror that Barbara inspired.

[II]

Patrick went to Edinburgh, found employment in a lawyer's office, and began to pay his addresses to a 'young gentle-woman'. By June of 1702 Barbara had followed him there, armed with a packet of his love-letters to her, and had managed to bring her story to the ears of the Lord Advocate, Sir James Stewart of Goodtrees. She apparently approached him through his wife, whose name was Agnes Traill and who seems to have been a distant cousin of Patrick's. Sir James listened, doubtless weighed the evidence of the letters, and gave his opinion that it was 'impossible' for Patrick to avoid completing his marriage with Barbara.

Patrick must have heard of this, for he now took a desperate step. He gained access to the house where Barbara was staying, searched her chamber for his incriminating letters, and eagerly snatched them up. Unluckily, he encountered Barbara on his way downstairs and attempted to pass her without speaking. In immediate suspicion she ran into her room, discovered the loss of the letters, hurried to the Lord Advocate and procured from him a warrant to arrest Patrick for theft. He was seized in his bed at midnight, Barbara herself accompanying the messenger, and clapped into the Tolbooth.

Next day, 25 June 1702, Patrick was brought before the Lord Advocate, while Barbara stood by. It must have been a terrifying interview. Sir James Stewart, who had risked his life for his principles more than once in the troubled years of the preceding century, was a stern, austere old man, now grown so fat that he could hardly rise from his chair without help; but his mental energy was unabated and he was the last man to pass over what he judged to be an attempt to cheat a wronged girl. He questioned Patrick at length. When he demanded what reason Patrick had for declining to marry Barbara, Patrick replied that as his father, on whom all his prospects depended, was opposed to the marriage, 'it would tend to both their ruins'. Barbara immediately retorted that 'she would take her hazard of that' and declared herself quite able to deal with Patrick's father and all his family. Before her inflexible determination and the Lord Advocate's frown, Patrick gave way and agreed that he would marry her.

He hoped for immediate release on the strength of his promise, but the Lord Advocate had not done with him. He summoned his confidential clerk, Thomas Spence, to draw up a declaration of the marriage on the spot. The document lies today in the Register House in Edinburgh, a small piece of paper, some six inches across and two and a half high, incongruously unimpressive.[1]

'I, Patrick Traill of Elsness,' it begins, 'doe hereby declare that I am willing to marie and doe actually take for my wife Barbra Fea, daughter to Patrick Fea of Whitehall, upon whom I begott a child under promise of mariage. And I the said Barbra doe hereby accept of him to my husband. And we obleidge us to solemnize this our mariage in face of holly kirk as the law prescribes, without prejudice of this our contract of actuall mariage *de presenti*. . . .'

Whether Patrick realized that by declaring his marriage before witnesses he was legally contracting it is uncertain. But he signed the paper, in slow, deliberate characters, and Barbara added her own signature pressing close on his. The Lord Advocate himself, Spence, and another clerk witnessed the declaration, and Barbara took the precious paper which had cost her such trouble to obtain and the very next day formally registered it in the Books of Council and Session.

But the days went by and Patrick showed no sign of making any arrangements for a religious marriage ceremony. So Barbara resorted to a combination of force and blandishment. The registration of the contract had made it a decree of the Court of Session, and Barbara now took the step of raising letters of horning against Patrick—that is, of having served on him the Court's injunction to carry out his promise. At the same time she gave Patrick to understand that this was just a formality, so that he should neither resist the order nor panic and leave Edinburgh. The next episode shows that she had the power of fascinating as well as frightening.

On 28 July, the necessary legal interval of fifteen days having elapsed without Patrick's having obeyed the Court's order, Barbara secured a warrant for his arrest and imprisonment. As luck would have it, a former school friend of Patrick's one Nicoll Nisbet, got wind of this, and hurrying to the Signet

[1] Register of Deeds (Durie), vol. 99, Part I, pp. 412–3 and warrant thereof.

Office found the messengers actually waiting there for the completion of the warrant. He rushed to Patrick's lodgings, found him absent, searched the streets for him, and finally came on him in a shop, sitting with its master and mistress and— Barbara Fea. The quartet were 'taking ane bottle of ale, and were very good company', Barbara's plan being clearly to hold Patrick in play till the messengers, armed with the warrant, should arrive and seize him. But Nisbet, not omitting to give Barbara a piece of his mind, dragged Patrick away, hid him in the Cowgate while they discussed what to do, and at ten o'clock that night saw him safely out of Edinburgh on horseback for Kelso, on the road to London. Fortunately Patrick had borrowed 200 merks from two Kirkwall merchants six days before, and so had money in his pocket.

He was in London by 11 August, proposing, as he wrote to his father, to sail for the East Indies in a merchant ship. Evidently he felt that the width of the world was not too much of a distance to put between himself and his wife. Instead he joined the Navy.

He served at sea for some years, being present at the capture of Gibraltar and the battle of Malaga Bay. Yet he was not safe from Barbara's pursuit even aboard a Queen's ship. It appears from one of his letters, though his narrative is far from clear, that at one stage Barbara actually reached Spithead and secured an interview with Patrick's captain, who, however, told her 'that she had come to the wrong person and likewise to the wrong kingdom'. Patrick, according to his own account, then managed to get Barbara arrested in London on what seems to have been a charge of vagrancy, and attempted to have her committed to Bridewell; but she obtained her release on bail and returned to Scotland.

'It cost me above £20 sterling for that base woman,' Patrick complained. 'Pray, dear brother,' he concluded, 'lett me have sum good hair by the first opertunity, for wigs is werie dear hear and hair with you is butt of a low price. Let it be as fair as posebell.' From which, though we know nothing whatever of

119

Barbara's appearance, we may conclude at least that Patrick's hair was tow-coloured.

[III]

Next year, 1706, Barbara changed her tactics. Apparently she had abandoned hope of securing the person of Patrick for her husband, but she was no less resolved to get her legal rights as his wife in his property. His father, John Traill of Elsness, had in 1696 granted to Patrick the lands of Housby in Stronsay, though reserving his own liferent in them and power to alter the disposition at any time. So, although Patrick had no possession of Housby, he had an interest in it which Barbara determined to realize for herself.

Late in the evening of 25 May 1706 she rode to Housby accompanied by her sister Kitt and two servants, and asked for a lodging for the night from the Traills' housekeeper there, Helen Jock. The request was granted. But next morning Barbara demanded the keys, and when Helen refused them struck her and took them by force. One of the farm servants later testified that he heard Helen crying 'Murder!' and saw blood on her face. Fortunately David Traill arrived, and with some difficulty persuaded Barbara to leave, although she was only too anxious to provoke him to drag her out of the house. 'She abused you, my mother and my selfe worse as I can express,' he reported to his father, 'all to irritate me for ane riot, but I did laugh att her.'

Barbara clung to the keys and took them away with her, so that the Traills had to change all the locks in the house. In July she descended on Housby again, gained entry by smashing a window with a hammer, broke open all the locks, and remained in possession for two or three days, declaring that she was Mistress of Housby. This time she had to be removed by a warrant of ejection from the Stewart of Orkney.

Defeated by Patrick in England and the Traills in Orkney, Barbara now transferred the battle to Edinburgh once more.

How she managed to perform these long journeys is a mystery, but she clearly had a persuasive tongue, and at all the stages of her lifelong persecution of the Traills seems always to have found people willing to assist her as a deeply wronged woman endeavouring to secure her rights.

In 1707, therefore, she raised an action in the Court of Session against John Traill and his son David for dispossessing her of Housby, claiming damages of £3,000 Scots (£250 sterling). She alleged that she had a right to the lands of Housby since they belonged to her husband, that she had been assaulted and unlawfully ejected from the house, and further, that the Traills had carried off from it both her husband's title-deeds and various bonds for money owing to him.

There was no substance in any of these allegations, but it cost the Traills some months and much trouble and money to refute them. In the end they were imploring the Court that 'a close may be put to this vexatious suit which has verie near ruined us with attendance and expence'. All the witnesses had to be brought to Edinburgh from Orkney, a journey of 260 miles by land, 'besides five several ferries'. The case dragged on from the late autumn of 1707 to the late summer of 1709 before the Lords finally pronounced in favour of the defenders. It was protracted by two contingent accusations. Barbara alleged that she, David, and some of the witnesses had all set out from Orkney together and that David had managed to desert her 'upon the hill of South Ronaldsay in a most tempestuous and stormy day of snow, on purpose that I might have perished', when she had only with great difficulty found refuge in a manse, where she lay sick for several days. By means of this subterfuge, Barbara claimed, David had reached Edinburgh and 'had his witnesses examined before I could come from Orkney'.

David claimed in his turn that Barbara had assaulted him in the Inner House, and that by law she should therefore lose her case forthwith. The Lords remitted it to Lord Grange to inquire into this. One witness deponed that while he 'was standing

121

hard by the said Barbara Fea at the little half door on the end of the bar in the Inner House, and David Traill a little space behind her, the said Barbara turned about to David, and called him a base thief, a robber and murtherous rascal, and wondered how he could look honest people in the face; upon which David Traill, clapping her gently upon the shoulder, said she was a modest woman, whereupon Barbara with the back of her hand gave him a stroak betwixt the mouth and the nose; upon which a bystander said, it was as good as a kiss'. Other witnesses said that David's nose did not bleed nor his eyes water, and that he 'continued smiling after he got the said stroak'. Barbara protested that David had been making provocative remarks and that it was 'no stroak at all but a thrust from me to be free of his bad language'. The Lords, upon Lord Grange's report, found the charge of assault not proven.

Barbara had one unshakable ground of action in that Patrick had acknowledged her as his wife and the law of Scotland upheld her as such. No worries about expense deterred her from further pursuit of the Traills, either; for she was 'poor Barbara Fea' suing *in forma pauperis*, in accordance with the humane old law of Scotland, dating from 1424, which directed that free legal aid should be given to 'ony pure creature that for default of cunnyng or dispenss can nocht or may nocht folow his causs'. Accordingly, she now proceeded to claim that John Traill, as liferenter of Housby, was bound to maintain his son's wife. The Court dismissed her petition on 31 January 1710. She attempted without success to reclaim—that is, to have the case retried—and then dropped the elder Traills for a time while she turned her attention once more to her missing husband. He had gone to Ireland, and was now living with another woman, one Esther Pottinger, as his wife. Having run them to earth, Barbara returned to Scotland and to the Court of Session. On 24 July 1712 she secured a decree of aliment against Patrick for 200 merks Scots a year (a little over £11 sterling) since Whitsunday 1703, the term at which he was held to have deserted her. For the next six years she carried on a series of actions against John Traill to force him, in default of Patrick, to pay her this annual sum.

One attempt was made during these years to bring about a peaceful composition of the dispute. Sir James Stewart of Goodtrees—the son of the Lord Advocate, who had died in 1715—advised John Traill to try to be reconciled with Barbara. Sir James pointed out that Patrick must inevitably inherit Housby, which would then have to bear Barbara's claim for aliment, and that 'your son must either all the days of his life abandon his native country or acknowledge her for his wife', while his offspring by his Irish wife must be regarded as illegitimate and so incapable of inheriting anything from him.

In 1718 Barbara returned to Orkney with a letter from Sir James, apparently prepared to discuss terms. But when she arrived there her violent temper flared up again and wrecked the scheme. Once more she broke into Housby, once more she beat the housekeeper and seized the keys; 'and when', wrote John Traill, 'I came out of Sanday to Stronsay to commune with her, she in a high, rude, and violent manner broke up the chamber door where I lay before I gott up, and attacked me with her female sharps, her nails, which eagle-like she fastned in my face by way of morning salutation'.

It was hardly surprising that no reconciliation took place. A year later John Traill's son-in-law wrote from Edinburgh: 'I cannot really express what fatigue and trouble she has put me to this winter session—her cause being noe less than 24 tymes called in the Outer and Inner House and by bills. . . . I must tell you her mallice is so great and furious that I dare scarce venture in the chamber or Parliament House if she be in it.'

During these years David Traill was trading as a merchant abroad, some of his letters being written from Bergen, Emden, and Amsterdam, and Patrick was trying, not apparently very successfully, to make a living near Belfast. 'I wish to God,' he

wrote to David in 1718, 'you could conveniently come here and
see me since I cannot come to you.' It was not only fear of
Barbara that kept him from returning home, but fear of the
law. The Court of Session's decree of aliment against him still
stood, and his Irish marriage was of course bigamous under
Scots law. However, he did once at least venture to visit his
parents in Sanday with his Irish wife, and this rash action put
a new weapon into Barbara's hands.

In the summer of 1719 Patrick undertook a voyage from
Ireland to Norway, and took his wife Esther with him. They
put in at Kirkwall and went to Sanday, where Patrick was at
last able to introduce Esther to his family, who thought her 'a
sensible discreet woman'. Oddly enough, only a few days before their arrival, Patrick's daughter by Barbara, Jean Traill,
who was now seventeen years old, had taken it into her head to
join her father in Ireland and without a word to anyone had
taken a passage from Kirkwall to Belfast. She evidently inherited her mother's initiative if not her temper; but the result
of her impulsive departure was that she missed her father and
apparently never met him thereafter.

Patrick and Esther stayed at Elsness only for a few days,
but that was enough to give Barbara the victory she had so
long sought just as it seemed to have eluded her. On 17 February 1719 the Court of Session, despite the long series of
arguments that Barbara had brought forward, had at last
given its decision that John Traill was 'not bound to aliment
his son's wife, he not having consented to the marriage'. But
Barbara now had a starting-point for fresh litigation, and she
secured a judgment that John Traill, having entertained his
son 'and a woman whom he called his wife', had encouraged
Patrick in his desertion of Barbara and so rendered himself
liable after all for her aliment. In 1722—the year in which
Barbara's brother James Fea of Whitehall, 'a gentleman of an
enterprising spirit', introduced the practice of kelp-burning
into the Orkneys—the Court of Session gave John Traill the
choice between putting Barbara in possession of the lands of

Housby or paying her 200 merks a year for her life from Whit-sunday of 1722. Rather than lose Housby to Barbara, John Traill decided to pay.

[IV]

Early in 1723 Patrick Traill died. By his testament he left his wife Esther an annuity of £40 sterling out of the lands of Housby (which could not possibly be paid and, in fact, never was), and a sum of £20 to Jean, whom he described as 'my bastard daughter Jane'. That independent young woman had by this time married one Thomas Neill, an exciseman, by whom she had a son, Patrick.

Patrick Traill's death did not by any means extinguish Barbara's feud with his family. Arguing that his interest in Housby had now descended to her as his widow, she claimed that that property should now provide her 'terce', that is, the liferent of one-third of her husband's heritage to which by the law of Scotland every widow is entitled unless otherwise provided for. When John Traill and David Traill both died in 1729, possibly worn out by the worries of a quarrel that had now continued for a quarter of a century, she transferred the suit against David's son and heir, another John Traill, who was a boy of ten, and his tutors and curators.

The leading Traill defender was now David's widow, Elizabeth Baikie (incidentally a niece of Barbara's), and the chief ground of defence was that John Traill the elder, exercising his right to alter his disposition of the lands of Housby to Patrick, had, since Patrick's death, granted them to David. Moreover, John Traill had in 1724 granted to David the lands of Elsness. The whole family estate to which young John was now heir was burdened with the maintenance of John Traill's second wife and her children, not to mention young John's mother, Elizabeth, and her six other children; and, as may well be imagined, old John Traill had left behind him considerable debts.

After another four years of litigation, Barbara in 1734 obtained a judgment awarding her the rents of the lands of Housby, and uplifted them to the tune of 3,250 merks (about £180 sterling). She also obtained an award of 600 merks in satisfaction of her terce, but John's curators continued disputing this for several years.

Further complications were caused by the intervention of Barbara's daughter Jean. In two elaborately argued processes, which the Court ordered to be conjoined, Jean and her cousin young John were each claiming, through their grandparents' marriage contract, to be heir to their great-grandfather, old John Traill's father and the first laird of Elsness, who had died in 1690. In 1736 the Court held that John, as heir male, was to be preferred to Jean, the heir whatsoever, and Jean's reclaiming petition in 1737 was apparently dismissed. At this stage Barbara herself died, on 30 March 1737. Her testament dative (which mis-states the date of her death as 13 March) was recorded on 19 July 1739. The only property it mentions is a bond for 2,000 merks owing to her by Sir James Stuart of Burray, dated 10 September 1735. The executor dative is her daughter Jean, 'lawfully procreated betwixt the said deceased Patric Traill and his said umquhile spouse'.[1]

All the original parties to this apparently interminable quarrel were now dead; but the end was not yet. In 1740 Jean gave up to John her claim to the lands of Elsness and also renounced her rights to her mother's claim of terce, in return for a cash payment of £105 sterling—which John had to borrow. Matters thus seemed to have ended amicably at last. But after John died on 4 December 1759 the apparently dead embers began to smoulder yet again. John left three daughters, and it was a question, on which they sought counsel's opinion, whether, in terms of old John Traill's marriage contract, the succession now fell to Jean's son Patrick Neill—who was in a good way of business as printer to the University of Edinburgh —failing male heirs of both Patrick Traill and his brother David.

[1] Edinburgh Testaments, cii.

Patrick Neill protested that he was averse to entering into a long litigation. But he had been chafing at the thought that his mother had given up her rights 'all for the paultry consideration of £105 sterling', and he had enough in him of his grandmother Barbara's blood to raise an action in 1761 against his three second cousins for production of all documents relative to the estate of Elsness, which property he reckoned to be worth £1,000 sterling.

This process dragged on for a few years, but finally, in 1766, Patrick Neill accepted a sum of £350 sterling in full satisfaction of any claim he might have against the estate, and a letter of 18 July of that year from one of the girls' curators reported that everything was concluded. It was sixty-four years since Patrick Traill had signed that small piece of paper which had had such ruinous consequences. His grandson, Patrick Neill, lived till 1788.

[V]

Thus far was the story of Barbara Fea and her legacy of litigation known to me in 1938. Although her spirit impelled the whole affair, even after her daughter and grandson succeeded her in it, yet her figure had lost some of the remarkable vividness with which it appeared in the early stages of the tale. I felt it tantalizing to know so little of her behaviour in her later years, and nothing of the manner or circumstances of her death. One highly characteristic letter, written a short time before it, at least showed that she never lost interest in securing her pecuniary rights. It was written to her niece, David Traill's widow, in these terms:

'ELIZEABETH,
Thes ar to aqainte you that I am in toun wantes my monay ye owe me and desiress ye may give it me as soun as pospell for I most heave it to pay some off my crided. Is all from your ante

Kirkall the 28, 1735.   BARBARA FEA.'

127

There survives also a letter, dated 28 January 1736 and addressed 'To Mrs Traill att her lodging in the Parliament Close', from an Edinburgh woman, Christian Carre, whom Barbara had evidently been pressing to pay a small debt. The writer describes her efforts to raise the necessary cash and then concludes desperately, 'If you will nott wait till Munday do as you thinke fitt'.

The last chapter in Barbara's story turned up quite unexpectedly. It was in 1954, and—of all places in the world—in my own home. I was going through a drawer of family papers when I came on a bundle of which the top document was docketed 'Will: Seton's about Mrs Trail's legacy.' The name 'Trail' surprised me, and it was still more surprising to discover that 'Mrs Trail' was none other than my old acquaintance Barbara Fea.

William Seton was a Writer to the Signet. He and his wife had known Barbara for a good many years: he referred to her as 'my honest old friend Baby Fea', and his obvious affection for her is one of the indications that she must have had, after all, quite an amiable side to her character. To these old friends Barbara's thoughts turned as death drew near. In her last years, it seems, she had been on bad terms with her daughter Jean, perhaps resenting her intervention in the litigation which had been, so to speak, Barbara's life's work. 'My wife and I,' observed Mr. Seton later, 'both pleaded more in her behalf than we got thanks for from her mother.' On her very deathbed Barbara, unforgiving to the last, devised a scheme to disappoint Jean of any legacy she might naturally expect on her demise.

It is astonishing, considering the life Barbara had led, that she had so much property to dispose of. Some of it was in the form of bonds. There was a little landed property in Stronsay which her brother, James Fea of Whitehall, had given her in 1726. This consisted of a house, called 'the Hall', with a 'yaird' or garden measuring 100 feet each way: the house had been in ruins in 1726, but Barbara had apparently managed to rebuild it, for in 1740 it was specifically described as 'new'. Instead of bequeathing this snug little property to her daughter, Barbara decided to leave it to charity. Some furniture she had in Kirkwall and had not used for years she would bequeath to Mrs. Seton. Her money should go to someone with no claim on it whatever.

It is impossible to know what whim moved Barbara to leave the Hall to the minister of St. Peter in Stronsay and the kirk session thereof as trustees for the poor of the parish—for there was in fact no such parish. St. Peter had been one of the three old parishes into which Stronsay had formerly been divided, but the island now formed the single parish of Stronsay. However, in due course Mr. Robert Scollay, minister of Stronsay, took sasine of the property as 'serving the cure of St. Peter',[1] so the bequest was not invalidated as it might have been, and it is to be hoped that the poor of Stronsay benefited from it.

It is necessary to go back a few years to explain how Barbara Fea came to be mixed up with my family. In 1722, when she secured her annuity of 200 merks from John Traill because he had 'entertained' Patrick and Esther at Elsness, one of her counsel was a youngish bachelor advocate from Ayrshire named James Fergusson (my great-great-great-great-grandfather). Mr. Seton, as a law agent, had often employed him in those days and subsequently, and they had always remained friends. Fergusson apparently showed Barbara some kindness beyond his professional services: in the contemporary phrase, he 'took her by the hand'. Fifteen years later she remembered him. He was now happily married, with a growing family, a baronet and a Lord of Session. When Barbara lodged in the Parliament Close she must have seen him passing on his way to the Court from his house nearby in Kilkerran's Court, Forrester's Wynd. Perhaps she had been invited there and taken a liking to his children. At any rate, she now decided to leave her money to his second son, James, a boy of six, and failing him

[1] Orkney and Zetland Sasines, ix, ff. 261–2.

to the eldest daughter, Jean, a girl of nine; and she executed the disposition only a few hours before she died.

Lord Kilkerran (as he was now styled) was somewhat embarrassed, as well he might be, by this windfall. With a wish to be just to both Barbara's disappointed daughter and his own children, he kept a bond of 1,200 merks for little James and allowed Jean Traill and her husband Thomas Neill, the exciseman, to make up titles to all the rest of the legacy; and in 1750 he immediately agreed to a request from Patrick Neill, their son, to be allowed to draw the interest on the bond. Little James never inherited it, for he died before his seventh birthday. His sister Jean, when she came of age, made Patrick a present of it, and my bundle includes a letter from his mother acknowledging Jean's 'great goodness and generosity'.

The dispositions executed by Barbara Fea as she lay dying in her lodgings in Leith, independent and implacable to the last, were four in number. My bundle includes that in which she left her money to young James Fergusson, signed not only at the foot but also in the margin, where she ordered to be inserted a small contemptuous afterthought of a legacy to her daughter 'out of charity'. If the charity is distinctly questionable, both the signatures are perfectly firm.

But the real discovery in the bundle was a long letter to Lord Kilkerran from Mr. William Seton, giving a full description of Barbara's end. It fills in the portrait of this astonishing woman so completely that I cannot conclude better than by giving it in full.

Edinburgh. 2^d. April 1737.

'MY LORD,

'I design'd to have writt your Lordship by last post, but was detain'd at Leith till after 8 at night at the chisting [i.e. coffining] of poor Baby Fea, who died Wednesday's morning, and to whom I, this day, saw the last duty done, as recommended to me under her own hand. However I apprehend Lady Jean, whom I had the honour to wait on before I went to Leith, Thuesday, would write your Lordship that night the

130

6. Lord Kilkerran

account I gave her Ladyship of Mrs Trail's settlement, in gratitude to your Lordship.

'This day sen'night, twixt 7 and 8 at night, a man whom I have but lately discover'd to be her daughter's husband brought me a message from her, to go and see her at the point of death, and to receive instructions from her, as to settling her affairs. I accordingly went, and found her in such case as probably not able to outlive next day. However she, most pointedly and distinctly, caus'd me loose the cords from about a trunk of hers, after setting it upon a chair before her bed, and having unlockt it with her own hand, she gave me out some papers,[1] quhairof she keept a note writt by my son. Her orders I began to execute on Munday's morning by one of the clock, and betwixt 4 and 5 was with her in her room at Leith, with her instructions extended on stamped paper, to that purpose. She specially assigned to your Lordship for Mr. James, his heirs &c, and failzieing him, to your daughter Mrs Jean, and failzieing her to any of your Lordship's children you shou'd please name, twelve hundred merks principal with annualrent and penalty contain'd in a bond granted to her by Archibald McLachlan merchant here and John Maitland late lieutenant in Lord Mark Ker's regiment, and two thousand merks with annualrent and penalty in a bond to her by Sir James Steuart of Burray. By another paper she makes over, in the same manner, all her moveable effects, with the burden of the payment to her daughter of twelve hundred merks, when so much of the effects free shall be recover'd, and nominates Mr. James her sole executor and universal legator &c.

'After reading to her these papers she caus'd adject on the margin of the general disposition, that she gave the 1200 merks to her daughter out of charity, and further burdened it with payment to Sir James Steuart of Burray of three hundred merks, the cause quhairof, she said, he wou'd know, when he heard of it, and on both reserv'd a power to herself to alter,

---

[1] Two of these survive among a box of Mr. Seton's correspondence now in the Register House (Letters of William Seton, W. S., 1707–60).

innovat, legate &c. Thereafter she caused me draw, beside her self, a paper making over to my wife some household furniture, bed and table linnen, body cloaths &c, left by her in the hands of some people in Kirkwall and gave her some things from her own hand. All this was done on Munday.

'I was indeed straiten'd in one thing, which was the disponing of a house and yard in the parish of St Peters to the minister and kirk session thereof and their successours for the behoof of the poor of that parish, which, to my great surprize, she was likewise able to sign, on Tuesday, and told me her daughter would not, nor durst not quarrell it. On Wednesday morning about 6 or 7 she died, and, by reason of my Lady Arnistoun's burial yesterday, I could not possibly get hearse and mourning coaches for burying Baby till this morning, that I saw her decently inter'd beside my own children in Grayfriers Church yard. She sent me eight guineas, being what she had by her, towards defraying the charges, for so far.

'I forgot to tell your Lordship that the general disposition is burden'd with the payment of her funeral charges and of her just and lawfull debts in so far as she ows, which I apprehend are very inconsiderable. I never indeed saw any person embrace death with better courage, nor more distinctness and resignation.'

9

The Appin Murder Case

In the late afternoon of Thursday, 14 May 1752, Colin Campbell of Glenure, a half-brother of John Campbell of Barcaldine and a Crown factor on the forfeited estate of Charles Stewart of Ardsheal, was shot from behind by an unknown assassin on the road through the wood of Lettermore, near Ballachulish ferry in Argyll, while on his way to order the eviction of certain Ardsheal tenants. James Stewart in Aucharn, a natural brother of Ardsheal's and the leading tenant on the estate, one of several people suspected of complicity in the murder, was arrested on 16 May and brought before the circuit Court of Justiciary held at Inveraray the following September, charged with being art and part in the crime. But it was Allan Breck Stewart, a kinsman of James (who had been his guardian), who was generally believed to have been the actual assassin. He was a deserter from the Army, had been 'out' in the Jacobite rising of 1745–6, and since then in the French service, but had visited Scotland several times as an emissary of the exiled and forfeited laird of Ardsheal, on which occasions he had often stayed at his guardian's house. He slept there, indeed, on Monday, 11 May, three days before Glenure's murder. On Wednesday and Thursday he was seen hanging about the ferry which Glenure was bound to cross, or wandering up and down the neighbouring burns with a fishing-rod. A few hours after the murder he brought the news of it to a house in Glencoe and spoke of his intention to flee the country, which he did, after sending to James for his clothes and for money.

In all the circumstances and in the light of his character, it is not surprising that Allan was formally indicted as the principal in the murder, and outlawed upon his non-appearance. He may well have been the assassin, and the account of the Barcaldine family in Burke's *Peerage* still lays Colin Campbell's death categorically at his door. Meanwhile, James Stewart, after a trial lasting for more than three days, was on 25 September found guilty art and part and condemned to death. On 8 November he was hanged near Ballachulish ferry and his body afterwards hung in chains on a conspicuous knowe near by.

Such is the outline of the famous Appin murder case, which attracted much attention at the time, is well remembered in West Highland tradition, and is known to almost everybody, though with its outlines considerably distorted, through having supplied the background to the plots of Stevenson's novels *Kidnapped* and *Catriona*. Like most people, I first heard of it through reading these stories, at the age of ten or so. Not till much later did I discover a sort of hereditary interest in it, by study of a family tree unusually crowded with lawyers. One great-great-great-great-grandfather, my direct ancestor and namesake, was one of the three judges who signed James Stewart's death-warrant. Another, George Brown of Colstoun, was the advocate who made the final plea in his defence. This family interest was further stimulated by my being led, on the occasion of the bi-centenary of the murder in 1952, to examine the original records of James Stewart's trial, preserved with the records of the Court of Justiciary in the Register House, and a quantity of contemporary correspondence connected with it—much of it, particularly many important letters among the Hardwicke and Newcastle MSS in the British Museum, unpublished. During that year I also visited every spot in Argyll connected with this famous murder.

These studies made me question the well-established tradition that James Stewart was wholly innocent of complicity in the murder, and that he did not have a fair trial. My statement of these doubts in an article in the *Scotsman* on 3 May 1952 provoked a furious correspondence in that journal's columns lasting for three weeks and showing once more how much dearer to the popular mind in Scotland is the preservation of legend than the desire for historical truth.

For this particular tradition has very deep roots. It began with James Stewart's speech at the gallows foot, which there is much reason to believe he did not compose himself,[1] and which was immediately printed as a broadside and assiduously used as propaganda against the Government of the day, having a particularly brisk sale in Edinburgh.[2] The official publication of the trial was undertaken partly in reply to this broadside, although indeed the Lord Advocate (William Grant of Preston-grange) had suggested it the day after the trial ended in a letter to the Lord Chancellor (the Earl of Hardwicke). He foresaw clearly enough the point on which the propagandists would seize, but was equally confident that the full story of the trial was a sufficient answer to it. 'I should be glad,' he wrote, 'to know your Lordship's opinion as to the expediency of publishing this trial, that the Jacobites may not have room to say, that the Government or the Campbels (for of necessity, to get a good jury, the greater part were of that name) have taken away a man's life without sufficient evidence'.[3]

Hardwicke referred the project to the Duke of Argyll, Lord Justice-General, feeling 'that it ought to be left to the discretion of his Grace and the other judges who tried the prisoner', and Argyll and his brethren, 'after mature deliberation' and partly on account of the wide circulation of the prisoner's 'dying speech', agreed. But the Duke had doubts. 'Nothing,' he wrote to Hardwicke, 'would there appear but mere matter of record, *viz.* the forms of proceedings and the depositions of the witnesses, the verdict and the sentence, whereas several things were said *hinc inde* during the tryal which an English reader wiuld be curious to see in print, which would be very

---

[1] British Museum: Add. MSS 35,447, f. 299; 35,450, ff. 223–4.
[2] *Ibid.*, 35,450, ff. 225, 230.   [3] *Ibid.*, 35,447, ff. 286–7.

difficult now if not impossible to supply, there being no such thing as short hand writers in this country, so that we might have possibly a pamphlet war disputing what was said or not said at the tryal.'

This exactly described the bare record of the trial as it appears in the minute book of the Western Circuit and the process. But steps were taken to supplement them, and Prestongrange intimated the progress of the publication in a letter to Hardwicke of 30 December: 'Part of it is already sent to press. . . . The counsel on both sides have agreed to make up from their notes and memorys the speeches and arguments—*hinc inde*—which I have no doubt may be done exactly agreeable in substance to what pass'd—and my own part of it I shall forthwith set about during these holidays.'[1]

The Duke himself did not contribute to the volume, but his final exhortation to the prisoner was reconstructed from the memory of several: no one had taken notes of it. Nothing however was put down of a long speech that he had delivered in the course of the trial, to which I shall make reference later. The depositions of the witnesses were printed from their summaries in the official record but, after the first two, not printed in the order in which they were taken in court; certain spellings in the original record were altered; and there were naturally a few misprints. These departures from strict accuracy were reproduced in the *State Trials* reprint and reappeared in David Mackay's edition of the trial published in 1907 and reprinted in 1931. Mackay, surprisingly, professed himself unable to find the original record and took his text from the publication of 1753, adding a few small errors of his own. The many valuable appendices to his work are marred by extremely careless and inaccurate transcription of the letters quoted, besides many omissions, some of them important, from their text.[2]

[1] Add. MSS 35,447, ff. 288–9, 295–6, 301, 309.

[2] *The Trial of James Stewart* (*The Aspin Murder*), edited by David N. Mackay. (Notable British Trial series. Butterworth: London, 1931.) For convenience I refer frequently to this well-known volume, but quotations are corrected from the original documents whenever possible.

But the Jacobites had the last word. Almost immediately after the official publication of the trial there appeared *A Supplement to the Trial of James Stewart*, by 'A Bystander', which, after many circumstantial allegations against the propriety of the trial, culminated in the question, 'Answer me now, good reader—was not this man m——d?'

To the 'dying speech' and to the *Supplement*[1] can be traced most of the accusations concerning the unfairness of James Stewart's trial. Accepted as facts instead of the *ex parte* statements that they mostly are, they have subsequently coloured legal as well as historical tradition. The learned Baron Hume conceded that there had been 'some unusual and indeed censurable circumstances in the manner of conducting' the trial.[2] Hugo Arnot had already detailed them, the first legal authority to do so, in 1785.[3] 'He was unfairly tried,' Lord Cockburn wrote in his journal in 1845.[4] Omond, writing the biography of Prestongrange in *The Lord Advocates of Scotland* in 1883, went far beyond Hume and Arnot, declaring that 'the proceedings were from the first unfair' and 'cannot be too strongly condemned'.[5] Stevenson's romance *Kidnapped* appeared three years later, followed by *Catriona*, and, adding the grace of literature to the weight of reputable opinion, gave the tradition new and enduring vitality. Mackay's editing of the trial scarcely pretends to impartiality on this question and certainly shows none. More recently the Hon. Lord Cameron, though without any new research into the subject, has given as his opinion that 'the scales of justice were deliberately tilted against' Stewart;[6] and Lieut.-Gen. Sir William MacArthur, basing himself confidently on uncertain ground, has, though crediting the

[1] The one reprinted complete and the other in part by Mackay, *Trial*, pp. 292-7, 331-41.

[2] *Commentaries on the Law of Scotland, respecting Crimes*, 1844, i, p. 282.

[3] *Criminal Trials in Scotland*, pp. 192-3, 225-9.

[4] *Circuit Journeys*, p. 278.

[5] G. W. T. Omond, *The Lord Advocates of Scotland*, ii, pp. 54-7.

[6] *Scottish Historical Review*, xxxiii, p. 99.

circuit judges and the Lord Advocate with sincerity and fairness, laid charges of cooking the evidence against the private prosecutors.[1] That the tradition of judicial murder still exists and is fervently maintained is shown not only by the correspondence in the *Scotsman* already mentioned but by a reviewer of Sir William MacArthur's book. This writer claimed, with a vehemence quite inappropriate to Sir William's own temperate reflections, that the book had proved James Stewart's execution to be 'a judicial murder, approaching, though not equalling, in enormity the massacre of the Macdonalds of Glencoe'.[2] Since that episode, sixty years before the Appin murder, was a military execution on secret orders without any process of law, against people not even accused of any crime, this fantastic comparison merely shows what hysteria with reference to the Appin case sentimental Jacobitism can inspire even today.

[II]

To consider with any profit the fairness or unfairness of James Stewart's trial, it is essential, first, to see the figures of the story in the light of eighteenth-, not twentieth-century ideas—and ideas moreover of the uneasy mid-eighteenth century, not of the tranquil age of David Hume and Adam Smith; and secondly to switch off the romantic glow shed on Jacobites and ex-Jacobites by the genius of Scott and Stevenson. The materials for investigation are, first, the official record of the trial itself preserved with the records of the Court of Justiciary in the Register House; secondly, official and semi-official Government correspondence there, in the Public Record Office, and in the British Museum; thirdly, contemporary private correspondence, especially that of the Campbells of Barcaldine, the Campbells of Stonefield, the Mackays of Bighouse (from which family Glenure's wife came), and Lord

[1] *The Appin Murder and the Trial of James Stewart*, 1960.
[2] *Times Literary Supplement*, 6 January 1961.

Milton, a former Lord Justice-Clerk and an intimate of the Duke of Argyll;[1] and fourthly, contemporary press references, all conveniently printed by Mackay.[2] Jacobite family correspondence would be interesting too; but Jacobite families tended to write few letters and keep fewer.

This evidence shows the leading figures in the story in a light very unfamiliar to those who take their history from tradition or from fiction, or who affect to regard all Campbells as the Nazis regarded Jews. Colin Campbell of Glenure, to begin with the murderer's victim, appears as a distinctly amiable man,[3] honourable, generous, and straightforward in his dealings, who on his death was the subject of an affectionate elegy by the famous Gaelic poet Duncan Ban Macintyre. 'The Red Fox'—a term once applied to him by Alan Breck, and borrowed by Stevenson—was not his common by-name, but 'Colin Roy'. His acceptance of the Crown factorship on the forfeited estates of Mamore and Ardsheal did not signify a tyrannous or grasping character: it was in the still respected tradition of simple country gentlemen who wish to make themselves useful in their own countryside. Prestongrange observed to the Lord Chancellor in a letter of 30 November 1753: 'The whole salary of the poor gentleman's factory, for doing the duty whereof he was assassinated . . . was no more than £10 10s. 7½d. per annum —which made me wonder how he accepted of it and was told for answer, that those forfeited lands lay in his neighbourhood, and he did not love to be idle.'[4]

Allan Breck ('Spotted Allan') we have to recognize, not as the engagingly humorous character of Stevenson's imagination but as 'an idle, fair-spoken, clever rascal',[5] a deserter from the

---

[1] Most of this is now in the Register House but many Barcaldine letters are in the National Library of Scotland, which also recently acquired the Fletcher of Salton MSS which contain Lord Milton's correspondence.

[2] *Trial*, pp. 307–15.

[3] See A. C. Fraser, *The Book of Barcaldine*, pp. 61, 76–7.

[4] Add. MSS 35,447. f. 301.   [5] A. C. Fraser, *op. cit.*, p. 67.

Army, a wastrel and sponger of whom one witness at the trial remarked that he had only once known him do a day's work.[1] It is worth noting that the prosecution produced five witnesses, two of them Stewarts, who testified that their own immediate suspicions after the murder had fallen on Allan Breck, and two more witnesses—one being Alexander Stewart of Invernahyle—that such was the common belief of the neighbourhood.[2] This throws a strong light on Allan's reputation. He was the likeliest person in Appin to have shot an unarmed man in the back.

Allan's appearance is vividly reported. James Stewart himself, who, though 'he hoped in God Allan Breck was not guilty of the murder', apparently believed he was, and denounced him five days after the murder in a letter still extant, described him as 'a desperat foolish fellow . . . a tall pockpitted lad' with 'very black hair'; and one of Glenure's brothers, more precisely, as 'about 5 feet 10 inches high, his face much marked with the small pox, black bushy hair put up in a bag, a little in-kneed, round-shouldered, has full black eyes, and is about 30 years of age'.[3] Stevenson, it may be noted, altered all these details except the smallpox marks, a reminder that he completely changed the character as well.[4]

The two circuit judges, Patrick Grant, Lord Elchies, and Sir James Fergusson, Lord Kilkerran, were both outstanding for their knowledge of the law; and the 'perfect probity and sincere regard for justice' of the one and the 'probity and integrity' of the other are vouched for by Lord Woodhouselee in his *Life of Lord Kames*. Both had been to Inveraray on circuit before, Lord Elchies more than once. The Duke of Argyll, Lord Justice-General, who also sat on the bench, was a trained lawyer, and by nature a stickler for legal proprieties.[5] It was not he, as many believe, who took the principal judicial part

[1] *Trial*, p. 164.   [2] *Ibid*., pp. 146–8, 152–3, 183.
[3] *Ibid*., pp. 148, 211–12, 308.   [4] *Kidnapped* (1886 ed.), p. 72.
[5] See my *Argyll in the 'Forty-Five*, pp. 22, 34, 45, H.M.C., *Polwarth MSS*, v, p. 60.

in the trial but Lord Elchies, the senior of the two circuit judges. Elchies also presided over the examination of thirty-six witnesses, Kilkerran of sixteen, Argyll only of ten. Colin Campbell of Skipness, the chancellor or foreman of the jury, was 'a very sensible man and bred an officer', of proved public spirit.[1] To the character of William Grant of Prestongrange, the Lord Advocate, who headed the prosecution for the Crown, Lord Woodhouselee paid a tribute which Grant's own extant correspondence shows to be just: 'There was in him a rectitude of moral feeling, and a principle of virtuous integrity, which regulated the whole of his conduct; and these, accompanied with a candour of judgment, a liberality of sentiment, and a winning gentleness of manners, were the pure offspring of a warm and benevolent heart. These qualities shone conspicuously in his discharge of the office of King's Advocate.'[2] The machinations to suppress evidence for the defence ascribed to him in Stevenson's *Catriona* are not merely wholly fictitious: they are wholly incredible.

But despite the characters of all these good and just men who played leading parts in condemning James Stewart to death, there persist several popular beliefs, many but not all traceable to *Kidnapped* and *Catriona*, that his trial was unfair.

The principal of these beliefs is that James was really done to death by the Campbells because he was a Stewart. In support of this is, first, the fact that the prosecution was officially at the instance of Janet Mackay, Glenure's widow, 'with the concourse of His Majesty's Advocat for His Majesty's interest', and that the Crown evidence was almost entirely gathered by the vigorous investigations of the Barcaldine family—who were after the trial repaid by the Government the very considerable expenses they had incurred. In all this there was nothing unusual. Sir William MacArthur's book makes

[1] *Argyll in the 'Forty-Five*, pp. 192, 245–6: *The Lyon in Mourning*, ii, p. 99; iii, pp. 190–1.

[2] *Memoirs of the Life of Lord Kames*, i, p. 40.

much play with discrepancies between the evidence given in court and the precognitions on which it was based, of some of which he discovered an unattested transcript in the National Library of Scotland. But precognitions are not evidence; and, since hardly any man will give exactly the same statements on any subject on different and especially on widely separated occasions, discrepancies are perfectly natural. Precognitions are *ex parte* statements, often not given on oath, not taken before a judge nor in the presence of the accused, and not, like court evidence, subject to cross-examination by the other side. Hence they are never permitted to be produced in court, and once the indictment has been prepared (after which no more precognitions can be taken) are usually destroyed.

The precognitions in the Appin case are not, of course, verbatim statements but the *précis* of the examining magistrates. Even as historical as opposed to legal evidence, their substance cannot reasonably be accepted in preference to that of sworn testimony given in court, modified in cross-examination, and digested by the impartial mind of the presiding judge who heard witnesses and counsel and signed his own *précis* of the evidence.

Other facts always brought forward as evidence of unfairness are that the Lord Justice-General who sat with the two Lords of Justiciary on the bench was the Duke of Argyll, the chief of Clan Campbell, and that eleven of the jury of fifteen were of his clan and name. It is implied or even alleged that the Duke took an unorthodox and unwarrantable advantage of his position as Lord Justice-General, and that the jury was 'packed' with a scandalously high proportion of Campbells in order to secure the conviction of a Stewart. Clan enmity, in short, is held to have swayed and corrupted justice.

Other allegations of unfair treatment of the prisoner are that there was delay in serving the indictment on him and hindrance of his preparations for defence. Sir William MacArthur has made yet another, certainly a novel one and entirely his own. The first day of the trial was taken up by a debate on the

142

relevancy of the libel, and 'these pleadings, on the part of the prisoner', says Arnot, 'were extremely ill-judged',[1] as they gave the Crown counsel the opportunity of bringing forward in advance several points of their case and so of reinforcing whatever impression the carefully detailed indictment might already have made on the jury. The plea of irrelevancy was quite properly repelled, and the Court found 'the lybel relevant to infer the pains of law . . . that the pannel James Stuart was guilty actor or art and part . . . but allow the pannel to prove all facts and circumstances that may tend to exculpate him and remit the pannel . . . to the knowledge of an assize.' This was normal procedure, form, and language in such cases, as Sir William MacArthur could have discovered by reading a few more justiciary cases of the period; and his statement that it 'could not fail to prejudice the jury still further against this much ill-used man'[2] is as baseless as would be the suggestion that a modern landlord's formal notice to quit a farm as a preliminary to the revision of its rent could prejudice the security of the tenant.

Lastly, it was suggested by Arnot and has been often repeated since that the trial should have been held not in Inveraray but in Edinburgh, where, it is supposed, a jury would have had no prejudice against the panel.[3]

To take the last point first, the authorities seem to have briefly considered the possibility of a trial in Edinburgh, but for a different reason—doubt whether any Highland jury would ever convict a Highlander. But both Argyll and the Lord Advocate assured the Lord Chancellor that an Argyll jury would be impartial—'as any jury in Middlesex or Mid-Lothian would be', added the Advocate.[4] James Stewart in his dying speech complained of several circumstances about his trial but not of its location. To demonstrate the gravity of the crime libelled—the murder of the King's factor in the execu-

[1] *Criminal Trials in Scotland*, p. 193.   [2] MacArthur, p. 57.
[3] Arnot, p. 229; cp. *Trial*, p. 16, MacArthur, p. 84.
[4] Add. MSS 35,447, ff. 235, 252.

tion of his duty—the western circuit town, which was also the chief town of the shire in which the murder had been committed, was the obvious place for the trial. This was freely admitted in court by Robert Macintosh, one of the counsel for the defence, who also said that he did not think the place of the trial could be any disadvantage to his client.[1] Moreover many of the witnesses spoke only Gaelic, and although their evidence was Englished for them by sworn interpreters there were plain advantages in having a jury most of whom could understand all the witnesses. There would have been great difficulty in bringing so many witnesses to Edinburgh. In any case, the prisoner would have gained nothing by being tried before a Lowland jury which would certainly have felt no tenderness for a Highlander with a record as an active rebel. Given the atmosphere of 1752—a point which must always be kept in mind—probably no jury in Scotland would have escaped the reproach of James's dying speech—'The bulk of the jury thought I had some foreknowledge of the murder . . . [and] gave in their verdict upon the prepossessed notion of guilt.'[2]

There is however no indication at all that the jury's verdict was against their consciences. The evidence was, as the prosecution recognized from the beginning, only circumstantial, and in the light of the modern belief that the verdict was inevitable and even pre-arranged, it should be emphasized that the prosecution by no means counted on it. 'I am afraid the proof will be scrimp,' wrote Barcaldine two months before the trial after the precognitions were complete.[3] The Lord Advocate was not without anxiety lest 'the trial should miscarry', but assured the Lord Chancellor that 'no care shall be wanting on my part'.[4]

Undoubtedly the prisoner did not get the facilities to prepare his defence that he should and in our own day would have had, but we must once more remember the strained atmosphere on 1752 in which an admitted Jacobite and former rebel,

[1] *Trial*, pp. 77–8.   [2] *Ibid.*, p. 295.   [3] *Ibid.*, p. 351.
[4] Add. MSS 35,447, ff. 235, 270.

accused of a serious crime with a strong flavour of sedition about it, would get no more than the bare letter of his rights. Delay in preparing the indictment there certainly was, but not deliberate and not more than was natural considering that over 700 witnesses were precognosced and that the Lord Advocate drew it up at unusual length. The full precognitions did not reach the Lord Justice-Clerk till 11 July, nearly two months after the murder and only two before the trial. 'I was sorry to be told by him,' wrote the Lord Advocate to the Lord Chancellor, 'that the discoverys are not great against any of the persons we have in custody. I shall however peruse them carefully, and consider what can be made of the evidence'.[1] A month later he had barely finished his task. Sir William Mac-Arthur's statement that 'it is incredible that the Lord Advocare could have seen' the precognitions, and that 'no doubt the indictment was handed to him ready made' is fanciful.[2] On 13 August the Lord Advocate wrote, 'I have been this afternoon drawing up my criminal libel against James Stewart.'[3] Thereafter it had to be printed, and a copy was served on James on 21 August. 'The law of Scotland,' as the Lord Advocate had mentioned to Lord Holdernesse in another connection on 23 June, 'allows the prisoner fifteen days after serving him with the indictment to prepare for tryal.'[4] Even with the change in the calendar which brought on the trial eleven days sooner than it would otherwise have arrived, James had nineteen days to consider his defence, and the prosecuting counsel, the Advocate excepted, no longer to prepare their own speeches.

In the Duke of Argyll's presence on the bench and in the composition of the jury there was nothing at all unusual. Inveraray had been included in the Western Circuit of the Court of Justiciary only since the passing of the Heritable Jurisdictions Act of 1747, before which time it had lain within the Duke's jurisdiction as Hereditary Justiciar of Argyll. The

[1] Add. MSS 35,447, f. 235.   [2] MacArthur, p. 66.
[3] Add. MSS 35,447, f. 270.   [4] Public Record Office, S.P.54, No. 42.

Duke had supported the Bill in the House of Lords, saying that he had always been ready to surrender his own rights of jurisdiction and that he thought the general abolition of such rights would on the whole be a benefit to Highland landlords.[1] At each autumn circuit since then—in 1748, 1749, 1750, and 1751—he had regularly sat with the circuit judges by right of the office of Lord Justice-General which he had held since 1710. He did not of course only do so at Inveraray. In July 1752 he had sat and voted with other judges in a civil case, 'the great claim' of Lady Mary Drummond to the forfeited Perth estates;[2] and if James McGregor alias Drummond had not broken jail the Duke would have taken part in his trial the following November.[3] His absence therefore at the autumn circuit of 1752 would have been much more remarkable than his presence. Mackay's statement that 'he went in person to Inveraray to try this case'[4] is fanciful. The Duke's own home was the natural place for him to be in at that time of year, and he had in fact been there since 9 August and would have been there sooner but for the by-election of a Representative Peer in Edinburgh in July.[5]

Arnot's statement that 'in this case alone did a Lord Justice-General and a Lord Advocate ever make their appearance at a circuit'[6] is thus far from accurate. But the Lord Advocate's presence was the one really unusual feature in the case. It was not due to Government orders and certainly not to pressure from any Campbell quarter, for his own letters make clear that it sprang from his personal resolve.

Prestongrange was in Bath when the murder took place, and heard of it only when he returned to Edinburgh near the end of May. It was, he wrote later, 'my intention on the first hearing

---

[1] Omond's *The Lord Advocates of Scotland*, ii, p. 37.

[2] Add. MSS 35,447, f. 253.

[3] S.P. 54, No. 42, 18 November 1752.   [4] *Trial*, p. 16.

[5] National Library of Scotland: Fletcher of Salton MSS, B.K. to Lord Milton, 9 August 1752; Add. MSS 35,447, f. 227.

[6] *Criminal Trials in Scotland*, p. 192.

of it, to attend the trial my self wherever it should be taken';
and he had intimated this intention to the Lord Chancellor on
11 June, before he knew who, 'of those who now are, or shall
be taken up for it', would be brought to trial.[1] A month later,
after he had heard from the Lord Justice-Clerk that 'the
discoverys are not great against any of the persons we have in
custody', he realized the risks inherent in his resolve to
prosecute in person. 'It would cross the end I proposed by
that unusual diligence,' he wrote to Hardwicke on 11 July, 'if
the trial should miscarry—for then the greater solemnity in
carrying it on would but add to the triumph of the malefactors
and their friends—whereas a successful trial in those parts, that
had been carry'd on in the most solemn manner, would serve
to convince those barbarians, that they must either subvert
this government or submit to it.'[2] The event was to prove him
right, for no other Crown factor was murdered in the execution
of his duty.

As to the composition of the jury, in the only four jury trials
at Inveraray between 1748 and 1755, the number of Campbells
on the jury was respectively eight, eleven (the Appin murder
case), ten, and nine.[3] The proportion of Campbells on this jury
was therefore not unduly high, not nearly so high as that
among the Commissioners of Supply for Argyll (thirty-one out
of thirty-eight) at their sederunt of June 1751.[4] Juries in those
days were not settled by ballot but chosen by the judges out
of the eligible assizers who had been summoned, who were
always men of known position and standing. In Argyll such
men would naturally be mostly Campbells. 'I cannot fear any
partiality of the jury in favour of the persons accused,' the
Duke wrote to Lord Hardwicke on 22 July, 'but I have some
apprehension that in England some may observe the great
number of persons in the jury of the same name with the
gentleman who has been murdered.' Since at this date the jury

[1] Add. MSS 35,447, ff. 217, 286.   [2] *Ibid.*, f. 235.
[3] H.M. General Register House: Minute Books of the Western Circuit.
[4] Duncan C. Mactavish, *Inveraray Papers*, p. 73.

had not yet been chosen, those who believe the Duke to have improperly influenced the trial may claim this forecast if they will as blatant evidence that he had decided the jury's composition in advance. But the figures quoted above show that a preponderance of Campbells in the jury was to be expected. 'This,' the Duke continued, 'is unavoidable, unless the Sheriff should affectedly pick out other names, which will be not only difficult to do, but possibly dangerous in point of justice.'[1] Here, again, those who believe the danger feared was to a Crown verdict may draw this interpretation if they will; but what was obviously in the writer's mind, as in Prestongrange's when he referred to the 'necessity to get a good jury', was the need for men of weight, education, and experience of the world.

Of the forty-three assizers summoned to court at this circuit, twenty-three were Campbells. Care was taken, however, to exclude from the jury all who were kinsmen to the Barcaldine family.[2] Of the other assizers, two, Dugald Stewart of Appin and John Maclean of Lochbuie, failed to appear, and the judges accepted their excuses and remitted their fines. Appin's excuse was that he could not leave his daughter who was lying sick in Edinburgh. He had 'expressed great surprise and concern' on first hearing of the murder, and had been one of the local gentry who had assisted in James Stewart's arrest.[3]

[III]

The whole course and conduct of the trial are against the suggestion often made that the verdict was a foregone conclusion. It lasted, as the Lord Advocate observed afterwards,

[1] Add. MSS. 35,447, f. 252.
[2] Archibald Campbell of Levenside's letter, 25 July 1752, in John McGregor Collection (H.M. General Register House), No. 166.
[3] Minute Book; Barcaldine MSS; *Trial*, pp. 142–3.

'immoderately long'.[1] The whole of the first day's sitting, which began at six o'clock in the morning, having been occupied by the debate on the relevancy of the libel, the Court adjourned till five o'clock the following morning, when it resumed and sat without any further break for 'full forty-eight hours'.[2] The Crown produced 50 witnesses out of 151 available, the defence 12 out of their 102, besides cross-examining many of the Crown's. Prestongrange then addressed the jury, and was followed by George Brown of Colstoun, Sheriff of Forfar, the leading counsel for the panel. The judges did not at that date charge the jury, but Lord Cockburn, nearly a century afterwards, recorded a Parliament House tradition (it cannot be rated as more) that they were 'faintly admonished by Elchies and rather encouraged by Kilkerran'.[3] It was after seven o'clock on the Sunday morning, 24 September, when the Court rose at last and the jury were enclosed. About noon or a little earlier they reached their verdict and 'came abroad as usual'.[4] A deliberation of four or five hours on their finding was certainly not hurried. Verdict and sentence were given on Monday, 25 September. If, as is often alleged, James Stewart's condemnation had been decided in advance, it could certainly have been secured with less trouble, expense, and fatigue, and the mere demonstration of justice could have been equally impressive and much less tedious.

No one who reads the printed report of even a modern trial for which verbatim transcripts of everything said in court are available can gather from it the atmosphere of the court or what measure of conviction the evidence of witnesses carried to the ears, eyes, and minds of the jury. It is far harder to judge the atmosphere of a trial that took place more than two centuries ago. Of this trial moreover, as already noted, we have not even a verbatim record. Yet there is some contemporary testimony to the state of mind of judges, counsel, and jury in letters written immediately after the trial. Prestongrange

[1] Add. MSS 35,447, f. 287.   [2] S.P. 54, No. 42.
[3] *Circuit Journeys*, p. 278.   [4] Add. MSS 35,447, f. 282.

wrote two long accounts of it: one on 25 September to Lord Holdernesse, some parts of which Sir William MacArthur has printed,[1] and another on 26 September to Lord Hardwicke.[2] The Duke of Argyll also wrote, more briefly, to Lord Hardwicke on the 25th;[3] and Lord Milton, a former Lord Justice-Clerk and close associate of the Duke, who attended the trial as a spectator, sent, probably on 26 September, a short account to Henry Pelham which I have not traced and to the Earl of Breadalbane some observations on the trial of which a much corrected draft survives.[4]

'The evidence,' wrote the Duke, 'consisted altogether of circumstances but came out stronger than the Crown's lawyers imagined it would have done. He denied his accession to the murder with strong asseverations in answer to the exhortation I gave him, but I verily believe he is guilty, and we are all of opinion that many of his clan were privy to this murder. The strong menaces that were proved upon the prisoner had great weight with the jury together with a circumstance which is local to the Highlands, viz. the implacable hatred and revenge that never fails to arise when any tennants of a clan are removed to make way for strangers.'

'All the material facts in the libel were prov'd,' reported Prestongrange to Hardwicke, 'and some very material circumstances farther, which came out in the course of examining the witnesses. . . . The actual murder tho' charged was not prov'd to have been done by Breck, nor did we ever expect it should, as there were no eyewitnesses who saw him at that instant.' It was at this point that he went on to suggest the publication of the trial so that Jacobites might not 'have room to say' that there had not been 'sufficient evidence'.

Lord Milton, as an auditor of the trial but not a participator in it, gained a stronger impression of what the evidence had

[1] S.P. 54, No. 42; MacArthur, pp. 85–6 and a short passage on p. 54.
[2] Add. MSS 35,447, ff. 286–7.   [3] *Ibid.*, f. 282.
[4] Fletcher of Salton MSS: enclosed, with some other papers, in a cover addressed to Barcaldine and dated 'Septr. 1752'.

Lord Prestongrange,
Died May 2ⁿ 1764
aged 63,

7. William Grant of Prestongrange, Lord Advocate

brought out. 'The whole facts,' he wrote, 'that Allan was the actor and James art and part there set forth were fully proved and many further material circumstances illustrating these facts which enlivened the prooff. Strong threatnings of death were proved to have been uttered by the pannell against Glenure and afforded the strongest evidence of his guilt.'

The impressions of John Campbell younger of Levenside, one of the Crown counsel, coincided with Lord Milton's. 'The proof,' he wrote, 'came out very strong. That Breck was the murderer J. Stuart's own lawyers at last owned was proved sufficiently.'[1] The Earl of Leven, who had not been present, clearly gathered similar reports from those who had. 'By what I hear,' he wrote to Hardwicke on 23 November, 'the proof came out so strong as made it impossible for the jury or court to err.'[2]

These quotations make it clear that the evidence given in court *sounded* much more damning than it looks in cold print. For instance, the printed version of the trial, in which the evidence of the witnesses has been re-arranged by the editors presumably to make a clearer narrative, obscures the probable impact on the jury of the close of the prosecution's case. The last three Crown witnesses to testify were actually James Man, an innkeeper in Rannoch, Duncan Stewart, a Rannoch pedlar, and last of all Allan Oig Cameron in Alarich in Rannoch, Allan Breck's uncle.[3] These three each told of seeing Allan Breck early in the week following the murder when, having received money and his French clothes from James Stewart, he was fleeing eastwards. Allan Oig himself obviously suspected his nephew to be the assassin; and the last words the jury heard from a Crown witness were his testimony to Allan Breck's own conviction that 'he was very sure, were he apprehended, he would be hanged'. The production of these three witnesses as

[1] H.M. General Register House: Campbell of Stonefield MSS, No. 138.
[2] Add. MSS 35,447, f. 299.
[3] *Trial*, pp. 150–2, but the Crown evidence as there printed continues to p. 187.

the climax to the Crown case was well calculated to leave the belief 'that Allan was the actor and James art and part . . . fully proved'.

[IV]

There was never any suggestion that James Stewart was the 'actor' in the murder: he was condemned and executed as 'art and part'. His champions, including those who placed the inscription on his memorial at Ballachulish, assert that he was wholly innocent. But this involves denial that he was in any way accessory to the murder, which cannot be substantiated unless Allan Breck too can be proved fully innocent of any part in it.

'Whosoever, being in the knowledge of the mortal purpose, though contrived and imagined by another, shall lend immediate and material aid towards the execution, is thus involved in the guilt of murder,' says Baron Hume; and further —'The only other sort of accession is by things done after, and in pursuance of the homicide; such as concealing the dead body, approving the deed, harbouring the actors, or enabling them to escape. It is clear that, taken along with previous knowledge of the mortal purpose, or any instigation to commit the murder . . . assistance afterwards is a powerful circumstance in support of the charge of art and part. . . . Of this description was the noted case also of James Stewart in Aucharn, for the murder of Campbell of Glenure.'[1] Of all this, as we have seen, 'the proof came out very strong' and 'the strong menaces that were proved upon the prisoner had great weight with the jury'.

James had laid himself so open to suspicion by the imprudent threats against Glenure which he and his son were proved to have uttered on more than one occasion as to arouse 'violent presumptions' of his complicity in the murder as soon

[1] David Hume, *Commentaries on the Law of Scotland, respecting Crimes*, i, pp. 274, 281.

as the first inquiries into it began. It was he who uttered the sentiment which Stevenson adapted and put into the mouth of Allan Breck, 'that he would travel upon his knees to gett a propper opportunity of shooting Gleneur throw the head'.[1] Sir William MacArthur is at great pains to prove that this particularly vivid threat was fictitious and its terms extorted by force or fear from one witness, John Breck Maccoll.[2] But even if it was never uttered the proof of James's quarrels with Glenure and threats against him by no means rested on this one witness: there were six others.[3] Five more testified to similar threats on the part of James's ward, *protégé*, and associate Allan Breck.[4] There was other evidence of James's hasty tongue, too. Ewan Macintyre, a young shepherd from Glenduror, James's former farm, who had the previous year taken service with Campbell of Ballieveolan its new tenant, testified that James had 'challenged him for accepting thereof, and told him that he would be fit-sides with him, sooner or later, for doing it'—an expression which shortly afterwards the jury heard from the mouth of Duncan Campbell the innkeeper at Annat, who told how he had heard Allan Breck say 'twenty times over that he would be fit-sides with Glenure'.[5]

It was not through the precognitions of witnesses that the first intimation of James Stewart's threats against Glenure came to light. Rumour or gossip affirming them clearly started immediately after the murder, as is shown by two letters to Lord Milton written from Inveraray by Archibald Campbell of Knockbuy. The first, on 17 May, only three days after the murder, reported, 'It's said severals of these countrys threattend to get rid of Glenure, or that he shoud of them'; the second, on 19 May, intimated James's arrest and added, 'It's said

[1] Statement of John Breck Maccoll: Barcaldine MSS (National Library of Scotland). Cp. *Trial*, p. 186.

[2] McArthur, pp. 78–81. [3] *Trial*, pp. 158–62, 165, 169.

[4] *Ibid.*, pp. 138–41.

[5] *Ibid.*, pp. 159, 139–40. It will be remembered that the order of evidence was re-arranged for publication.

James Stewart was one of those who threatend geting rid of Glenure.'[1] So it was not unreasonable that the indictment laid stress on 'particularly the threatenings of death and destruction which the said James Stewart, and the said Allan Breck Stewart . . . have been heard to utter against the said Colin Campbell of Glenure, now bereaved of his life'.[2]

One of these threats by James may well have been made in jest, and another in drink;[3] and probably they were not serious. But it is certain that it was James's careless tongue that first brought him within reach of the law. No one could doubt then or doubts today that it was the Appin evictions in which Glenure was engaged that supplied motive for the murder, and James was the leader of resistance to them. His prominence in this character, in conjunction with the rumours mentioned by Knockbuy, perfectly justified his arrest on suspicion. Suspicion was greatly strengthened by the discovery that he had concealed illegal weapons in his house. But what really sealed his fate was his too ready response to a kinsman's need. After the murder, although James, like everyone else, believed Allan Breck to be the probable assassin, he none the less sent him money with which to leave the country and the suit of clothes that Allan had left at Aucharn. The discovery of this circumstance was, explained the Lord Advocate, 'the first thread which the kindred got hold of to lead them to a more full detection'.[4] Thus James could very properly have been convicted, and appropriately punished, for conspiracy to defeat the ends of justice; and in our twentieth-century view that seems to be the utmost penalty he should have suffered, especially since he was morally bound by the ethics of his race, class, and period to assist the escape of a kinsman who was in trouble with the Government.

But—once more—it was not the twentieth century. And apart from the assistance which James certainly gave to the presumed murderer after the fact, and from the question—to

[1] Fletcher of Salton MSS.   [2] *Trial*, p. 49.
[3] *Ibid.*, pp. 159–60.   [4] *Ibid.*, p. 116.

which his champions return an emphatic negative—of whether he gave assistance before the fact, there is the question of whether James had fore-knowledge of it; for, as Hume says, 'Taken along with previous knowledge of the mortal purpose, . . . assistance afterwards is a powerful circumstance in support of the charge of art and part.'

In the letter to John Macfarlane, W.S., which James wrote on 19 May soon after his arrest, stating his suspicions of Allan Breck and giving a description of him, he also stated the cirstance which helped to condemn himself: the general belief that 'it was a premeditated thing, to which I must have been knowing'.[1] That the murder was 'a premeditated thing' and that the purpose was known to many beforehand is beyond doubt. Rumours of this fore-knowledge had reached Campbell of Knockbuy on 17 May, as his letter to Lord Milton shows, and on the same day one of Barcaldine's sons wrote to him from Glenure, 'My poor uncle was several days ago forwarnd'.[2] On the 24th the Earl of Breadalbane, probably repeating what he had heard from Glenure's brothers, whom he knew well, mentioned to Lord Hardwicke that Glenure had been told 'that a resolution was taken to murder him' and 'advised to be upon his guard'.[3]

I shall discuss presently the evidence for a widespread conspiracy, but the question at the moment is whether James Stewart knew that an attempt was to be made on Glenure's life. To me this seems impossible to doubt. He was the acknowledged leader of the Ardsheal tenants, 'a sort of head of the family interest of Ardshiel since his attainder', as the Lord Advocate observed;[4] and he was on friendly terms with all his neighbours, many of whom, as much evidence at the trial showed, had loose tongues when in their cups. He must have known all the gossip of the countryside; and the imminence of an attempt on Glenure's life could not have been concealed from him if warnings of it had reached Glenure himself.

[1] *Trial*, p. 211. [2] *Ibid.*, p. 370.
[3] Add. MSS 35,450, f. 211. [4] *Ibid.*, 35,447, f. 270.

It is possible that he did not take the information seriously; probable that in any case he preferred to shut his ears to it. But his first words on hearing of the murder—'Lord bless me, was he shot?'[1]—strongly suggest a sudden and horror-struck recollection of something heard before and since then ignored; and his words and actions thereafter as reported by various witnesses are all consistent with those of a bewildered man realizing with sudden and appalling clarity the perilous position in which he had put himself by not denouncing the plot, by not himself warning Glenure of it, and by harbouring so recently the very man whom he realized to be at the heart of it whether or not he was the principal actor.

[V]

Legally, therefore, if it be accepted that James Stewart must have had some fore-knowledge of the murder, the verdict of 'guilty art and part' was quite correct. It was none the less James's misfortune rather than his fault that he incurred it, and in a modern trial this would certainly have been recognized. But the Crown had long ago decided that in the public interest punishment for murder must be inflicted and guilt not less than that of murder must therefore be brought home to one of those at least accessory to the crime.

This resolution was not prompted by mere vindictiveness. If it had been, young Allan Stewart would have been tried, and most probably convicted, as well as his father. Certainly a thirst for revenge is openly expressed in one or two extant letters of the Barcaldine Campbells[2] in their first outburst of grief for the death of Glenure, who left a young wife pregnant and two small daughters. His brothers took up the hunt for

[1] *Trial*, p. 172. John Beg Maccoll's evidence of James Stewart's first words on hearing the news is confirmed by that of the latter's own son Allan (p. 201).

[2] *Trial*, p. 370.

Allan Breck and his associates with the utmost determination, spending almost £1,200 (most of which they had to borrow) in the expenses of precognoscing witnesses and all the other charges of the prosecution. But it need not therefore be assumed that only the zeal of the Campbells brought James Stewart to the gallows, nor that his name doomed him. Of the many extant letters which passed between Argyll and Breadalbane Campbells at this time, not one hints at any animosity against the prisoner's clan. The one man who showed that animosity was the old Duke of Argyll in his final address to the prisoner, and it was not against Stewarts as Stewarts but Stewarts as rebels.

Yet James would have hung just as certainly if Glenure's name had been Stewart and his own Campbell, or both of them Smith. It was 'His Majesty's interest' that weighted the scales.

The point was not that Glenure was a Campbell but that he was a Government servant. Under the Act forfeiting estates belonging to rebels (25 Geo. II, c. 41), Ardsheal was one of the properties of which 'the clear rents' were annexed to be devoted 'to the purposes of civilizing the inhabitants upon the said estates . . . the promoting among them the Protestant religion, good government, industry, and manufactures, and the principles of loyalty, and to no other purpose whatsoever'. Ironically enough, the Earl of Leven was pointing out the good effects of this Act in a speech to the General Assembly, to which he was Lord High Commissioner, on the very day when Glenure was murdered. 'The forfeiture of the few,' he observed, 'is made subservient to the good of the whole, and the very weapons of rebellion are become the spring of true and lasting felicity even to rebels themselves'.[1]

Colin Campbell of Glenure and his elder brother John Campbell of Barcaldine were two of those appointed by the Barons of Exchequer as Crown factors on the forfeited estates 'with an allowance not exceeding £5 per cent. of the rental'. Both had

---

[1] *Scots Magazine*, xiv, p. 239.

served with the Argyll militia throughout the Jacobite rising of 1745–6, Barcaldine himself being one of eight Campbell officers who refused to draw any pay.[1] Their loyalty to the King could hardly be doubted: yet it was. In the years after the rising the Government trusted the loyalty of few Scotsmen and scarcely any Highlanders. Glenure had carried out the difficult task of Crown factor, which he accepted in 1749, with all the lenience he could. Half a Cameron himself, he had let a farm on the Mamore estate (which he also factored) to John Cameron of Fassifern, brother to 'gentle' Lochiel. He was reprimanded and received the strictest orders from the Barons of Exchequer to let no farms to any kinsmen of forfeited owners, nor to any who did not voluntarily take the oath of allegiance to the King. Despite their past services and the strong recommendations of Lord Breadalbane, who had also served actively during the rising,[2] both Barcaldine and Glenure were on the point of dismissal as suspected Jacobites when the fatal shot ended Glenure's employment for ever.

The immediate result, apart from clearing Barcaldine of all further suspicion, was extreme alarm and anger among the judicial authorities and the heads of Government. The Lord Justice-Clerk, Charles Erskine of Tinwald, on receiving 'two several expresses' reporting the murder, 'thought it greatly for His Majesty's service, that a rigorous and thorough inquiry should be made', issued warrants for the arrest of suspects, and sent appropriate orders to all the seaports: measures which he reported to Lord Holdernesse, the Secretary of State, on 18 May, the Monday after the murder.[3] The Lord Advocate's immediate reaction has already been mentioned. Meanwhile the Duke of Newcastle was in Hanover with the King. His brother Henry Pelham, Lord Holdernesse, and the Lord Chancellor Hardwicke all wrote to him on 28 and 29 May letters which show how from the very first news of the murder they regarded it not as an ordinary crime of violence but as a

[1] *Argyll in the 'Forty-Five*, pp. 127, 245. [2] *Ibid.*, pp. 39, 128, etc.
[3] S.P. 54, vol. 42.

deliberate act of rebellion. 'There never was a more daring attempt against a Government,' wrote Holdernesse; 'Your Grace may depend that no care or diligence shall be wanting on my part to bring the offenders to justice.' Pelham called the murder 'barbarous and audacious', and the Lord Chancellor styled it 'an audacious and outragious insult upon the Government . . . meant with a general view to intimidate their officers from putting into execution the laws relating to the forfeited estates'. The Lord Advocate, writing to Hardwicke a fortnight later, considered the murder, 'doubly audacious now, when that country is one object of the present attention of the Government and the legislature'.[1]

What was doubtless in all their minds was the embarrassing attacks that might follow in Parliament against the Government's policy, already criticized, of attempting 'civilizing the inhabitants' of the Highlands from the rents of the forfeited estates. Lord Breadalbane foresaw other effects. On failing to secure the services of a dairymaid from Northumberland, he observed in a letter of 25 May, 'The character of the Highlands must be low indeed when a person will not come from the north part of Northumberland to it. This murder will frighten all English people from coming amongst us beyond the Forth.'[2] This echoes Duncan Campbell's outcry on first hearing of his brother's murder—'The Government can expect to gat none to serve them in those barbarrows parts if they do not interest themselves in a most particular manner in this matter.'[3]

These phrases alone are enough to explain the offer of a reward of £100 sterling for the discovery of the murderer or murderers, the rigour with which the charge against James Stewart was pressed, the Lord Advocate's resolve to prosecute in person, and—in due course—the repayment by the Treasury to the Barcaldine family of the whole costs of the prosecution. Indeed the Barons of Exchequer were assured on 8 March 1753 that the murder 'being of so heinous a nature committed on an

---

[1] Add. MSS 32,727, ff. 276, 287–8, 290; 35,447, f. 217.
[2] John McGregor Collection, No. 11.   [3] *Trial*, p. 370.

officer of the Crown in the execution of his duty the expence was always intended to be defrayed by the Crown'.[1]

Pelham and Hardwicke both expressed regret for their former doubts of Barcaldine's and Glenure's loyalty; the order already signed for Barcaldine's removal was, with the King's approval, suspended, and Glenure's factorship was later bestowed on Mungo Campbell, his nephew and the witness of his death. Glenure, Pelham pointed out, had, 'in the execution of his duty, done well, and acted with spirit against the relations and old tennants of the forfeiting person, which was undoubtedly the cause of his being murdered'.[2]

But one man was hardly convinced even by Glenure's fate that Jacobitism was not rife among the Campbells. This was the Duke of Cumberland, with whom the Lord Chancellor had a long conversation on 10 June which he reported very fully to Newcastle. 'The Butcher,' having been in Scotland for six months in 1746, considered himself an authority on its people. His view in 1746 had been that 'the greatest part of this kingdom are either openly or privately aiding the rebels';[3] and in 1752 he still doubted whether any Scot could be really loyal to the Protestant succession. 'No body,' he assured Hardwicke, 'who has spent their life here, and has not been in that countrey and seen their practices, can have any notion of them,' and he 'own'd his suspicions' of both Barcaldine and the dead Glenure. Hardwicke replied with details of how the brothers had been 'educated from their infancy in Whig principles' and of their service with 'every relation and tenant almost' during the '45. 'These,' he pointed out, 'were pretty strong proofs'; but the Duke, it was plain, admitted them only with reluctance. 'He does not give up his point,' commented Newcastle, 'and I think continues his distrust, as to what will hereafter be done.'[4]

Cumberland, though he had some influence, had fortunately

---

[1] Public Record Office: Treasury Out-letters (Various), vol. 70.
[2] Add. MSS 32,727, f. 287.   [3] *More Culloden Papers*, v, p. 36.
[4] Add. MSS 32,727, ff. 406–7; 32,728, f. 92.

no authority; and the Government did not share his doubts
whether the law officers in Scotland would do their duty, even
though the Pelhams and the Duke of Argyll had been political
enemies for years. 'I hope,' Pelham had written to his brother
the Duke of Newcastle, 'you think we have done right here. I
realy think they are doing and mean to do right in Scotland.'
After the trial, on 6 October, he wrote, 'Our friends in Scotland
have done extremely well. The chief villain concern'd in the
murder of Glenure is convicted, and will be hang'd in chains
upon the spot, where the poor man was killd, as soon as the
law will allow. The D. of Argyle tried him himself, and the jury
were his countrymen, almost all Campbels.'[1] The Lord Chancellor was likewise convinced that the prosecution had been
carried out 'with great earnestness, and with thorough diligence and attention', though he greatly regretted that 'the
principal actor and more of the contrivers of that horrid fact'
could not be brought to justice.[2]

Thus James Stewart's life was exacted partly as a warning
to the disaffected of Appin and Lochaber but partly also as a
testimony of the loyalty to King George of the judicial
authorities in Scotland, not one of whom, except perhaps the
Duke of Argyll, was altogether free of suspicion by the English
statesmen who knew so little of 'North Britain' and had been
so badly frightened by the Jacobite rising seven years before.
But even without these political motives no one could have
considered allowing the brutal murder of a Government servant in a Jacobite district to go unpunished. It seemed clear
that the deed had not been the work of a single man and that
his accomplices had probably been numerous. The conviction
of one accomplice was to serve as a warning to all.

The processes of law were strictly respected. But it was not
thought improper in those days to apply coercion to timid or
unwilling witnesses. There were indeed some high-handed

---

[1] *Ibid.*, 32,727, f. 287; 32,730, f. 38.

[2] Letter of 25 November 1752 in Bighouse MSS (H.M. General Register House), No. 54.

measures in this case to ensure that the available witnesses should actually testify in court. Sentiments justifying such actions are to be found in a letter to Barcaldine from Colonel John Craufurd, commander of the Fort William garrison: 'In the short experience I have had of this part of the country, I have found that in order to come at the bottom of any villainy, many methods are necessary to be put in practise, to give the law an oportunity of exerting its force. . . . Therefor I have not scrupled to operate either upon the love, fear, interest or even revengeful spirit of the person who I meant shou'd be of use, when my intentions were that their discoverys shou'd produce a general good.'[1]

The pains taken to establish James's complicity in the murder were due, not to any personal animosity against him or his clan, but to the anxiety of the Government lest any appearance of lenience should encourage lawlessness in the West Highlands. There was a quite sincere belief that his death on the gallows at Ballachulish would 'produce a general good'.

[VI]

At the back of all these motives lies the conviction, which was certainly in the minds of judges, counsel, jury, and many witnesses throughout the trial, that a conspiracy shared by numerous people in Appin, and possibly in Lochaber also, lay behind the murder. Sir William MacArthur scouts this belief, holding that the only tenable theory is that the murder was 'an act of private vengeance' by 'a man so crazed by a sense of tyranny and injustice that he cared nothing for any consequences to others, so long as the oppressor could be struck down'.[2] Sir William's opinion, based on extremely careful study of the trial and the ground, deserves respect; but his theory is at variance not only with everything believed at the time but with some written evidence still extant though not all

---

[1] *Trial*, p. 372.   [2] MacArthur, p. 109.

in print. It is the firm conviction on the part of the Barcaldine Campbells that a conspiracy existed that explains the precognoscing of so many hundred witnesses. They were not merely looking for direct proof of James Stewart's complicity: they were trying to find the murderer's other associates—and of course the murderer himself. The same conviction explains the quite extraordinary assistance lent by the Army to the search, and the preoccupation of the Lord Justice-Clerk and the Lord Advocate.

From the very beginning of the investigations, Colin Campbell's murder was ascribed to more than a single criminal—to 'some damnd villans who fired att him out of a bush',[1] 'the contrivers as well as the actors',[2] 'the barbarous wretches, actor and accomplices',[3] 'some assassins, who . . . made their escape',[4] and so on. 'From Glenure's words and the situation of the place where I saw one of the villains, there's reason to believe there were more than one on the spot,' wrote Mungo Campbell on 23 May;[5] and in the official record of the account he gave in court of Glenure's last words—'Take care of yourself, for he is going to shoot you'—the words 'he is' are written on top of what was first set down as 'they are', proving that in either Mungo's mind or the clerk's the notion of more than one murderer on the spot still persisted even though his evidence described but one. 'We are all of opinion,' wrote the Duke of Argyll on the conclusion of the trial, 'that many of his clan were privy to this murder';[6] and Lord Milton's conclusion was: 'From the evidence it appears that the pannell is not the only guilty man as accessory to the murder but that it was known to most of the Stewarts in that neighbourhood, some of them instruments.'[7] Lord Breadalbane's summary on 1 November may be taken to represent the general opinion of the prosecutors: 'Many circumstances which appear'd at the trial, and others very well known, shew that the design was

---

[1] *Trial*, p. 370.   [2] *Ibid.*, p. 372.   [3] S.P. 54, vol. 42.
[4] *Edinburgh Evening Courant*, 21 May 1752.   [5] *Trial*, p. 305.
[6] Add. MSS 35,447, f. 282.   [7] Fletcher of Salton MSS, *ut cit.*

form'd a considerable time before it was executed, and that several persons were concern'd in it.'[1]

That many were in fact privy to the murder is the impression left strongly on the mind by a careful reading not only of the record of the trial but of the discussions of the crime and of the hunt for its perpetrators which fill so many contemporary letters. There is the sense of an 'underground', of a secret knowledge shared by many people and guessed at by many more, which the Highland genius for reticence kept undisclosed. Since the private prosecutors could not unearth the conspiracy no modern investigator can hope to do so. But that such a conspiracy, with many involved in it, did exist there is some evidence.

From the start there were rumours that more than one man had been present at the actual shooting of Glenure. Only one shot was heard, and the two bullets which passed through Glenure's body seem to have been fired from a single gun. But Mungo Campbell in his first recollections of the incident suspected that the murderer had not been alone. 'From Glenure's words,' he wrote, 'and the situation of the place where I saw one of the villains, there's reason to believe there were more than one on the spot, and circumstances concur in convincing us that there were numbers of Lochaber as well as Appin potintates in the combination.'[2] Within three days after the murder Archibald Campbell of Knockbuy had heard a rumour that Glenure's companions 'saw 2 men with a gun each, one whereof fired, run away, but could not know who they were'.[3] Another version of the same rumour appears in the evidence of John Breck Maccoll who met Allan Breck three days after the murder and, he said, told him that 'two poor women that had come up Glenco were telling that Glenure was murdered Thursday evening in the wood of Lettermore; and that two people were seen going from the place where he was murdered; and that he, Allan Breck, was said to be one of

[1] Add. MSS 35,450, f. 221.   [2] *Trial*, p. 305.
[3] Fletcher of Salton MSS.

164

them.'[1] Before 28 May the report had reached Fort Augustus that Glenure had been killed by 'two Highlanders'.[2] Two months later 'one of the Maccolls' had a story that the second man had been Allan Stewart, James's son.[3]

Whether or not the man seen by Mungo Campbell on the hillside just after the murder was Allan Breck Stewart, my own belief is that, although carrying a gun, he was not the man who had just fired the fatal shot. He was, I think, already too far above the road when Mungo saw him. In court Mungo was not certain whether it was before or after he helped Glenure from his horse that he himself ran up the hillside; but in the letter he wrote only nine days after the event he was quite positive that he 'started up the brae' as soon as he turned back on hearing the shot, and that 'Glenure still kept his horse' when he descended the hill to return to him.[4] The alternative —that he abandoned his dying uncle while 'he leaned a little upon the deponent's shoulder, and endeavour'd to have opened his breast, to see where the bullets, wherewith he was shot, came out of his body'—is against all probability; and moreover neither of Mungo's companions, who joined him within two minutes at most, saw him either 'starting up the brae' or coming down it.[5] Glenure's dying words—'Take care of yourself, for he is going to shoot you'—strongly suggest that he got a glimpse of his murderer, who, from the angle at which the bullets were fired, was certainly close at hand, not firing from high up the hill. Having studied the ground, I do not think it possible that the murderer, encumbered with a gun heavier that a modern rifle or shot-gun and not much shorter than himself,[6] could in the minute or so before Mungo saw him have got so far up the steep and uneven hillside 'that the deponent thinks he cou'd not have known him, tho' he had seen his face', was only vague about his clothes, and apparently could

[1] *Trial*, p. 182.   [2] *Ibid.*, p. 14.   [3] *Ibid.*, p. 384.   [4] *Ibid.*, p. 304.
[5] *Ibid.*, pp. 134, 136.
[6] I have handled a gun of the period which measured five feet two inches from butt to muzzle.

not see whether he wore a hat or a bonnet. I am bound to add, however, that Lieutenant Alastair Campbell of the Argyll and Sutherland Highlanders, who recently, as part of a Territorial exercise, carried out an interesting and valuable reconstruction of the murder on the actual ground,[1] considers that no definite deduction can be made whether the man Mungo saw was the actual murderer or not.

That the fugitive Allan Breck was the murderer was clearly believed by almost everyone in Appin and Rannoch, including his own uncle. In disbelieving that, as so many nowadays do, it must be borne in mind that we are opposing the opinion of those much better able to judge the probabilities than we are. If he was not the murderer, however, his conspicuous presence near the scene of the crime immediately before it, his almost ostentatious inquiry about Glenure's movements,[2] his former threats against Glenure (for which there is ample evidence),[3] as well as his instant flight, all show that he was involved in the affair, if not as a principal then as an accessory: perhaps as a supervisor, perhaps as a decoy.

Much has been said, not only by Sir William MacArthur, of the pressure put upon witnesses by the private prosecutors, examining magistrates, and officers at Fort William; but the private prosecutors themselves suspected much secret activity by those who knew the murderer's identity and were prepared to go to any length to suppress its disclosure. Barcaldine, after the precognoscing of some early witnesses, wrote of his 'good hopes of getting the villains . . . brought to justice in spite of all the pains that has been taken to make the poor wretches perjure themselves';[4] and John Breck Maccoll, one of the prosecution's key witnesses, was 'in vast terror of being murdered' by 'the Steuarts', having been warned by 'a gossip of his in Suna' that they were bent upon it, while at the same time he 'had offers of a reward if he would continue stanch to

[1] See his article in the *Weekly Scotsman*, 13 April 1961.
[2] *Trial*, p. 147.   [3] *Ibid.*, pp. 139–41.
[4] S.P. 54, vol. 42.

the Steuart interest'[1]. It is possible that the almost unanimous accusation of Allan Breck was intended—and even pre-arranged—by many who voiced it to avert suspicion from others. 'The way his name has been mentioned to me by the Steuarts,' wrote Colonel Craufurd from Fort William on 23 May, 'fully convinces me, that his name and absconding was intended as a peace offering for the rest of his friends.'[2]

The investigators certainly believed several people to be involved; and their correspondence shows that they had specific suspicions about various individuals, notably James Stewart's son Allan, John Stewart younger of Fasnacloich, Allan Cumming, a miller 'married to a Stewart and in great confidence with the Appin people',[3] and one Ewan Roy Maccoll, brother of John Breck Maccoll the bouman in Coalisnocoan.[4]

But these, from south of Loch Leven, were not all the suspects. Mungo Campbell and his kinsmen, it will be remembered, thought from the first that 'there were numbers of Lochaber as well as Appin potintates in the combination'; and the most probable of these to be involved was the 'gentle Lochiel's' brother, John Cameron of Fassifern. Lord Breadalbane had reported in November 1751 that Glenure was 'at the greatest variance' with Fassifern and was 'hated by the people of that country'.[5] Mungo Campbell discovered that Fassifern had employed Allan Cumming the miller as an agent 'to stop the tenants from paying their rents to Glenure' from the forfeited Mamore estate;[6] and on 9 July Duncan Campbell the Sheriff-substitute wrote to Barcaldine, his step-brother, as follows: 'I cannot help thinking that Fasfern knows as much of the plot which brought our brother to an untimely end as any man of his name whether the fact was committed by Stewarts or others'.[7]

In this letter Duncan Campbell alluded to the discovery of

---

[1] *Trial*, pp. 384–5.   [2] *Ibid.*, p. 373.   [3] *Ibid.*, p. 374.
[4] See MacArthur, pp. 67, 99.   [5] See MacArthur, p. 25.
[6] *Trial*, p. 374.   [7] *Ibid.*, p. 380.

'Blairmacfildich's dark correspondence with Fasfern' and to the existence of 'animosity' between Fassifern and Alexander Cameron of Glennevis which might possibly lead one of them to incriminate the other. Now it happens that a fragment of this 'dark correspondence' has survived, and guarded though it is it hints that a plot to get rid of Glenure was being discussed by Cameron 'potintates' nearly three years before his death. A copy only exists, without signature.[1] The writer was a Cameron, a cousin of Glennevis. His letter, dated from Blarmacfildach, about two miles south of Fort William, on 16 June 1752 and addressed to John Cameron of Fassifern, runs in part thus:

'Dr. Sir,—Three days ago I was summond in to be examined anent Gleneur's murder. I need not tell you the question they would propose to me or to any others if I had answerd them if you remember what you perpose the night that Culchena was buried. . . . I can not refuse but I hea[r]d breathing and not only that but propose of the same to my self to do. Therefore you must excuse me when it comes to the push for telling the thing that happened betuixt you and that night [sic].'

The missing word in the last sentence may have been 'me' but was perhaps some other name. After the funeral of Allan Cameron of Cuilchenna, Fassifern, Glennevis, 'and a great many others returnd to Culchena's house', on the headland on the north side of Loch Leven, opposite Ballachulish, and there 'took a hearty glass', the invariable custom at a Highland funeral. Fassifern had a violent quarrel with Glennevis and threw a glass of punch in his face; but, this incident apart, the above letter shows that during this evening there was 'breathing' of some proposal the revelation of which after Glenure's murder would have been awkward for Fassifern and others even though the incident had happened as long ago as August 1749. The writer however, for all his perhaps intentionally embarrassing hints, did not incriminate Fassifern in his precognition, but like other Camerons examined with him main-

[1] John McGregor Collection, No. 166.

tained that he 'knew of none that had any manner of hand in that murther by advice threatning or otherwise'.[1]

This trail evidently faded out, although the defence produced two witnesses, John Cameron of Strone and his servant, who swore to having heard a Cameron say that he would shoot Glenure 'if he met him in the high way'.[2] But no evidence could be found that this man, known as Serjeant More Cameron, had been seen anywhere in the district for many months before the murder.

Another trail which the prosecution followed with some eagerness but likewise without avail is the subject of one of the Appin traditions about the murder. Sir William MacArthur has dispassionately examined and exploded many of these traditions,[3] but on this particular one he is too sceptical. It tells that the conspirators against Glenure met in a lonely spot in Appin for a shooting-match, having agreed that the best shot among them should be the assassin and the best gun his weapon. Donald Stewart, says this story, the nephew and son-in-law of Alexander Stewart of Ballachulish, was the chosen man and actually shot Glenure, and the chosen gun, a long Spanish one, belonged to one Dugald Maccoll.

Now this legend, unlike some others, is certainly old, having been written down about a century ago when old men could still have remembered talking to contemporaries of the murder.[4] Sir William MacArthur has convincingly demonstrated the extreme improbability of Donald Stewart's having been the actual murderer. But there is some substance in the legend none the less, for several points in it, though not necessarily related, can be established as facts.

Dugald Maccoll was a servant of James Stewart's, and figured as an important Crown witness. Though he told much, including how he helped, during the evening just after the mur-

---

[1] *Highland Papers* (Scottish History Society), iii, pp. 47–8, 50.
[2] *Trial*, pp. 191–2.   [3] MacArthur, pp. 100–8.
[4] Dewar MSS at Inveraray Castle; typescript copy in the Register House.

der, to hide a long Spanish gun 'that used to stand in the brew-house' at Aucharn,[1] perhaps he did not tell all he knew. An unpublished letter from Barcaldine which can be dated 24 May gives a vivid glimpse of the taking of a precognition from him: 'I forgot to tell you that Dougal MacColl turn'd so faintish upon his second examination that the Shirriff call'd for water to throw on his face. But he recovered and stood stiff, tho' we all believed the murder would be out.'[2] It is probably to him also that Mungo Campbell alludes in a letter of 10 June, mentioning one of James Stewart's servants who 'is extreamly singular in his behaviour. He has been two or three times brought before the judge to be examind, and no sooner some questions were put to him than he fainted, and we could get no more speech of him. This fellow its hopd will soon make a clean breast'.[3]

Was Dugald on the verge of revealing something about a shooting-match? The investigators certainly learned about it from somebody, but very late in their inquiries, and could find nothing definite enough to be included in the indictment. A few days before the trial the words 'I much wish some thing coud come out of the shooting match'[4] show that after all nothing had done so.

Yet there were men in Appin who could have taken part in such a contest. James Stewart's wife, in the last of her three judicial declarations, owned 'that there was a gun in her husband's house this spring, which she saw her son Allan go out with once or twice to kill black cocks'. This was confirmed by John Beg Maccoll and according to Dugald Maccoll was on 'two or three mornings . . . in the latter end of March, or beginning of April last'.[5] Dugald Maccoll also gave evidence that 'Allan Breck Stewart was also in use to carry out the large Spanish gun to shoot black cocks'.[6] In the same month of

[1] *Trial*, p. 167.
[2] Letter to Colonel Craufurd, dated '3 o'clock Sunday morning', in S.P. 54, vol. 42. [3] A. H. Millar, *Forfeited Estates Papers*, p. 284.
[4] *Trial*, p. 386. [5] *Ibid.*, pp. 207, 173, 168. [6] *Ibid.*, p. 168.

April, only a few weeks before the murder, Allan Breck said to
the innkeeper at Annat, one Duncan Campbell, that 'he hated
all the name of Campbell' and told Duncan to tell 'his friends'
(*i.e.* kinsmen) 'that if they offered to turn out the possessors of
Ardshiel's estate, he would make black cocks of them . . . by
which the deponent understood shooting them, it being a common phrase in the country'.[1] It seems possible at least that
when young Allan Stewart told his mother that he was going
out to shoot blackcock he was really bound, on a more sinister
errand, for a lonely rendezvous where other young men with
guns were assembling, and that Dugald Maccoll well knew for
what purpose the long Spanish gun that he helped to hide had
formerly been taken out.

The prosecutors seem not to have unearthed allusions to the
shooting-match before July. On 28 July one of Barcaldine's
sons, Captain Alexander Campbell, wrote to his father that he
had been in Appin and Duror investigating it and hoped 'to-
morrow' to see 'young Lagnaha' and take 'proper steps to get
every thing he knows out of him as to the shooting match I am
still in the dark about, tho' I have not left a stone unturnd to
get att the certainty of it. Invernahyle,' he went on, 'quite
misinformed you as to the name of the place, there being no
such place as he told you in all Appin or Glenco. Leckninnamatan is the place, and I am told there is not the breadth of a
bonnet of plain ground in the whole if it.'[2]

On 31 July Captain Campbell wrote again to his father from
Glenure. 'As to the shooting,' he reported, 'I have got nothing
of [it], but if Invernahyle does his duty and follows the method
I proposed to him he must get a distinct account of it. The
place belongs to Salachoil. I can't help thinking that Duncan
in Insack[3] knows more than he has yet discoverd, and that
nothing but his wife's nephew Phasanacloich being so deeply

---

[1] *Ibid.*, p. 139.

[2] Letter dated from Dalfour printed in *Trial*, pp. 383–4, but with this
passage omitted.

[3] Duncan Stewart in Inshaig.

concernd hinders his making a clean breast. He seems to me to be a sagacious fellow, and I think it hardly probable that a thing of such consequence committed in his neighbourhood and by his next door neighbour, could be carried on without his knowledge of it beforehand; and I am certain he knows what share James['s] family have had in the real fact.'[1]

The place traditionally pointed out as the scene of the secret shooting-match is Lochan Blàr nan Lochan, though how Captain Campbell can have garbled it into 'Leckninnamatan' is a mystery. It lies hidden in the hills south of Glen Duror, 1,350 feet above sea level, nearly five miles from Salachoil which is in Glen Creran. All the people lately mentioned lived at distances near enough for it to be not inconvenient for a secret rendezvous. Young Fasnacloich's home was about three miles away. Aucharn and Inshaig were about four miles to the north, and Invernahyle about the same distance to the south. Two miles further than Aucharn, and on the road which Glenure would have travelled had he passed unhurt through the wood of Lettermore, was the house of Lagnaha. 'Young Lagnaha' was another Allan Stewart, younger brother to Donald Stewart of Achnacone and husband of Duncan Stewart in Lagnaha's daughter.[2] He too was illegally possessed of a gun.

A few weeks before the murder James Stewart's son and Allan Breck had both been out with a gun ostensibly 'to shoot black cocks'. James Stewart, at whose house Allan Breck habitually stayed, owned that gun and another, which it was illegal for him to possess. Young Allan Stewart had been intimate with Allan Breck and had lent him a greatcoat; and Allan Breck had seen much of James Stewart younger of Fasnacloich during the week before the murder and stayed three days at Fasnacloich house. Young Fasnacloich's uncle, Duncan Stewart in Inshaig, was another intimate of young Allan Stewart, and the latter claimed to have been at his house, only a few hundred yards from Aucharn, at the time of the murder

[1] *Trial*, pp. 384–5, with this passage omitted.
[2] *Ex inform.* Brigadier Ian Stewart of Achnacone.

and was in company with him the following day.[1] All these associations appeared suspicious, and since Colin Campbell of Carwhin, a Justice of the Peace who was present when the declarations were taken from the Aucharn family, was later one of the jury at the trial, their implications may well have been conveyed to the rest of the jury through him, quite apart from what was said in court. Moreover, despite the Disarming Act, the number of illegal firearms in Appin and Lochaber appeared to be considerable. Besides those seized at Aucharn, others kept coming to light during the investigations right into July; and even after the trial another, 'hastily cover'd over with grass and earth,' was found near the scene of the murder, and according to Lord Breadalbane was 'known to have belong'd to a son of Stewart who was executed'.[2]

So many Stewarts engaged on so many mysterious errands— so many concealed guns—so many people intimate with the disreputable Allan Breck whose headquarters had been at Aucharn! Yet despite all the precognitions no proof of a conspiracy was discovered. None the less a settled conviction that there must have been one must have been present in almost everyone's mind throughout the trial. It was felt that the principal instigators and actors of Glenure's murder, apart from Allan Breck, had not been unearthed, and that James Stewart stood at the bar merely as a single representative of them. The shrewd comment of an English reader of the printed trial in May 1753 must have echoed that of many in Argyll on James's execution—'that he saw plainly by the tryal above twenty-five people must have known of the murder, and that only one had been hanged'.[3]

[1] *Trial*, pp. 200–1.
[2] *Highland Papers*, iii, p. 49; Add. MSS. 39,450, f. 244.
[3] *Trial*, p. 362.

[VII]

This impression of a sinister cloud of secrecy hanging over the whole affair would be strengthened by the atmosphere of the time. This is particularly hard—though essential—for us to imagine today, when we are separated by well over 200 years from the last battle fought on British soil, when we feel no fear of rebellion or civil war, which to us are but phrases in history-books, and when we have no apprehension for the security of the Protestant succession, a matter of the very greatest concern to our eighteenth-century ancestors.

But this mental tranquility and sense of security did not exist in 1752. The ordinary Scottish citizen lived in what felt like a mere breathing-space between hurricanes. The political and religious oppressions of Charles II's and James VII's reigns were more or less within his parents' memory (any very old man or woman still living would be able to recall the Revolution). The last Jacobite rising—there had been two previous ones—had been suppressed only six years before. The sinister strength of France, which had financed and largely armed it, was no further away than the English Channel, and the Jacobite menace was by no means regarded as dead. Jacobite agents, as the evidence about Allan Breck's movements recalled, were passing freely between Scotland and France; and before James Stewart's execution the Lord Justice-Clerk had received reports from Fort William that 'McDonald of Lochgarry and Dr. Cammeron the late Lochiel's brother are come to the Highlands' and that 'in general the disaffected seem to have hopes given them from some quarter or other'.[1] The 'Elibank Plot' was brewing. The Government was purging the Customs service of 'supposed disaffected persons'.[2] The fear of a French invasion was, as in 1745–6, always in the background.

[1] Letters of 26 October, 6 and 21 November in S.P. 54, vol. 42.
[2] Add. MSS 35,447, f. 217; 32,728, f. 70; 32,730, f. 38.

It is in this light that the Lord Advocate's resolve to make every effort he could devise to secure an exemplary conviction must be viewed. He knew that the evidence was only circumstantial and he set forth as much as he could in the indictment. 'I thought it better,' he wrote to Hardwicke on 26 September, 'to give the jurors opportunity to peruse and consider at leisure the series of facts discover'd and ponder the weight of them, if prov'd, than to trust to their opinion form'd during the trial, which must be long and fatiguing . . . and on the other side it was also doing justice to the prisoner to let him know beforehand what presumptions of guilt he was loaded with, and had to explain for his defence if he could, that he might provide and bring his evidence accordingly—and I was glad to find that the event has proved that this method was right. . . . The prisoner was well and decently defended by the four counsel he brought.'[1]

The night before he had written, in a long letter to Lord Holdernesse, 'It is with great satisfaction to my self as it is to every body here, excepting the friends of the prisoner, that I am able to give an answer so satisfactory to your Lordship's letter as the trial was indeed of very great importance to the future well government of Scotland, and especially of the Highlands, and as justice so loudly required some vengeance or satisfaction for the murder of poor Glenure, who was basely assassinated whilst he was pursuing the duty of his office in the King's service, and for no other offence than his doing that duty.

'And I have further the satisfaction to inform your Lordship that this long and important trial was conducted on all sides with great temper and decency even on the part of the counsel and agents for the prisoner, as well as those for the King, and the kindred of the deceas'd.'[2]

In the same light should be regarded the assiduity of the

[1] Add. MSS 35,447, f. 286.
[2] S.P. 54, vol. 42. MacArthur (pp. 54 and 85–6) prints parts of this letter but omits about half, including the passage quoted here.

private prosecutors—further spurred, of course, by their affection for the murdered Glenure and his widow, who 'behaved like an angel' with remarkable 'prudence and resolution'.[1] So also should the notorious harangue of the old Duke of Argyll to the prisoner which has provoked so much shocked comment.

The Duke had in his lifetime witnessed three Jacobite risings in the Highlands, had been 'shot in the arm and side' at the battle of Sheriffmuir,[2] and had seen much of his property damaged or destroyed in the '45. None knew better than he the effects of these three revivals of seventeenth-century violence against the growing order of the eighteenth. He himself, like other heads of his family, had moved with the times. The '45 had interrupted his plans to build a new and well-designed town, and for himself a modern house (a castle only in name), at Inveraray. He had planted woods and improved farm lands. He was so modern in his outlook as to believe that 'it would be in reality a benefit to Highland landlords if the whole clan system were abolished'[3] which had facilitated, three times over in his lifetime, the raising of formidable private armies against the Crown. Now in his old age he saw in the murder of Glenure a sign that disaffection and the turbulent spirit of clanship still survived, and his whole nature and the tradition of his house rose in protest against them. His address to the prisoner, after touching on the '15, the '19, and the '45, reached its climax in the affirmation that 'this murder has been visibly the effect and consequence of the late rebellion'.

This conviction of the Duke's, amounting, it may be said, to an obsession, had been displayed much earlier in the trial when the prisoner's counsel wished to cross-examine Donald Campbell of Airds, one of the most respected men in Argyll, in order to prove from his mouth that the accused bore a good charac-

[1] Alexander Campbell's letter of 17 May: passage omitted in *Trial*, p. 370.

[2] Henrietta Tayler, *The Seven Sons of the Provost*, p. 73.

[3] Omond's *The Lord Advocates of Scotland*, ii, p. 37.

ter. The Lord Justice-General opposed this on the grounds, outrageous to the twentieth-century mind but understandable in a man of his time and outlook, that no one who had been a rebel could have a good character. This interposition is briefly mentioned in the *Supplement to the Trial of James Stewart* but is much more fully described in Lord Milton's letter of which the unpublished draft survives:

'The lawers for the pannell offered a prooff of the pannell's morall good character. The Justice-General was in court. His Grace told them that it was not usuall and always exposed the pannell to a prooff of the contrary, but as the lawers of the pannell insisted his Grace asked what character he had during the late rebell[ion] and it being answered and admitted that he was [a captain *deleted*] in the character of an officer among the rebells the Duke in a speech of near half an hour laid open the barbarity of the part uncivilised Highlanders, the restraints that had from time to time being [*sic*] necessary [to] subject [them], the wick[ed]ness of the rebellion, and concluded with showing that no rebell was intitled to a morall good character —which I assure you was of great and good use to the numerous auditory, for the tryall was carried on in the church, the court house being too little.'[1]

[VIII]

There are said to be people in Appin today who claim to know the real murderer's identity and also claim it to be their duty to keep it secret. It seems to me ridiculous to suppose

[1] Fletcher of Salton MSS. It is strange that Lord Milton's mention of the place of the trial should be the sole contemporary reference to it, finally settling a much-disputed question. The church was not the present one of Inveraray but that of the old town close to the old castle; it was a low building with no tower. The Duke was of course the only heritor in the parish, and his permission to use the church for a judicial purpose would be sufficient.

THE APPIN MURDER CASE

that silence can be thought to assist belief in James Stewart's innocence, since both he and Allan Breck Stewart must lie under the imputation of murder till proof or strong probability of the contrary can be shown. But in fact tradition, centuries after the event, is of little or no value for solving an historical mystery. Sir William MacArthur has demonstrated how little reliance is to be placed even on the genuinely old traditions crystallized in writing in the Dewar MSS a century ago; and much less can be placed on those allegedly extant today, after *Kidnapped* and many other writings on the Appin murder have started new trains of thought to seep into the popular mind.

If I am asked for my own view of the murderer's identity I can give only a tentative answer. That many people in Appin in 1752 were linked in a conspiracy to murder the King's factor is, I think, more than probable and was certainly believed by many much more able to judge than we today can ever be. That Allan Breck Stewart and James Stewart's son Allan were both deeply involved in it I believe; and my own guess at the actual murderer would light on young Allan—whose alibi seems to me suspect—with assistance from one or more of the Ardsheal tenants, perhaps John Maccombich the miller.[1] The reticence of witnesses who might have inculpated him could be amply explained by their knowledge that even if young Allan were convicted and hanged as the actual murderer his father would assuredly hang just the same as an accomplice, and Mrs. Stewart would lose a son as well as a husband. That James Stewart himself was morally innocent of the murder I believe; but that he was legally guilty art and part—from fore-knowledge (although inactive) combined with aiding the escape of a participant—I also believe. That the conduct of the trial was by eighteenth-century standards fair and proper I hope I have demonstrated; and the verdict has been approved by the impartial authority of Baron Hume: ' I see no reason to

[1] Grounds for suspecting the miller have been indicated by Lieut. Alastair Campbell (*Weekly Scotsman, ut cit.*).

believe that the verdict was not according to the justice of the case, or different from what the jury were warranted to return, on the evidence laid before them.'[1]

Popular opinion however has not got beyond the partisan one thus summarized in a letter of 10 October 1752 from John Campbell younger of Levenside, one of the Crown counsel in the case: 'The Jacks have espoused James Stuart's side of the question very keenly, and cry out loudly against the jury, witnesses, etc.'[2] That loud outcry, echoing over two hundred years, has drowned all sympathy for the original victim, Colin Campbell of Glenure, and all understanding of the motives of upright and public-spirited men whose only concern was justice, order, and the peace of a recently disturbed country. It has also drowned all reproach for the real villain of the piece, the still unidentified assassin through whose wicked and stupid action two good men lost their lives and two families were plunged into mourning.

[1] Hume, *op. cit.*, p. 282.
[2] Campbell of Stonefield MSS, No. 138.

10

The Fortunes of William Niven

As one of Robert Burns's boyhood friends in his Kirk-oswald days, William Niven has a definite if modest place in the poet's biography. To him were written, in 1780–1, the three earliest of Burns's letters known to survive. Another, of 1786, shows that Burns's affection for him lasted into manhood. 'Mr. William Niven, merchant, Maybole' was among the subscribers to the first Edinburgh edition of Burns's poems. It is said that 'subsequently they fell out', and that in later life Niven claimed that it was to himself that Burns's *Epistle to a Young Friend* had originally been addressed —despite the facts that the 'young friend' is specifically named as 'Andrew' and that Burns and Niven were almost exactly of the same age.[1]

Possibly these traditions are groundless. Hardly any of Burns's biographers have traced Niven's successful and to some extent distinguished career beyond his early association with the poet. A generation ago a minister of Kirkoswald, Mr. James Muir, who gathered much information about Burns's Kirkoswald friends into a small book, thus summarized Niven's later life:[2]

'William Niven, it is said, acted as partner with his father, and afterwards as sole partner, in the business at Maybole. On the death of two bachelor brothers in Jamaica, he became possessed of the immense wealth which they had amassed

---

[1] *Letters of Robert Burns*, ed. Ferguson, i, pp. 1–4, 39; ii, p. 363.
[2] *Robert Burns till his Seventeenth (Kirkoswald) Year*, p. 79.

8. William Niven

there—£100,000, it is said—and purchased the estate of Kirk-bride, near Maybole. Nevertheless, he became hard and par-simonious to a degree. At the mature age of 85, he died 13 December 1844, and lies buried in Maybole churchyard. His portrait, long hanging on the walls of Kirkbride House, is now to be seen in Maybole Town Hall.'

This is not altogether accurate, and a rather fuller account of William Niven can be drawn from information unknown, though mostly quite accessible, to Mr. Muir. As with all biography, the public records are the obvious, though often neglected source. There are also allusions to Niven in the *New Statistical Account of Scotland*, and a small bundle of his letters survives among the Hamilton of Pinmore papers in the Register House.

Niven was born in February 1759, the second son of John Niven by his wife Janet Spear. He spent almost his whole life in or near the little town of Maybole. His father was a shop-keeper there and also owned the small neighbouring farm of Kirklandhill. William himself prospered as a merchant and later as a banker. There was some foundation, as I shall show, for the story of the Jamaica inheritance; but like many legacies this one was much smaller in fact than in tradition. It was Niven's industry, with the encouragement and help of a local laird, not the death of rich brothers, that raised him to pros-perity and ultimately wealth.

Precisely what help Niven received in early life is uncertain, but it came from Hugh Hamilton of Pinmore, the purchaser of the Pinmore estate in the Stinchar valley. The late owner had been Robert Kennedy of Pinmore, who sold it in 1781;[1] he had been one of the many Ayrshire lairds ruined by the collapse of Douglas, Heron & Company's bank in 1773. James Hunter, who had been their cashier, founded, with the help of his brother and two cousins, the new banking business of Hunters & Company which, much more prudently conducted, flourished for seventy years and was finally merged in the Union Bank of

[1] Register of Deeds, vol. 230 (Mack.), f. 115.

Scotland. Of this bank Hugh Hamilton was one of the direc-
tors; and since Niven became its Maybole agent he presumably
owed this position to Hamilton's patronage.

At any rate, Niven constantly and gratefully acknowledged
the assistance he had had in early life from Mr. Hamilton. In
1810 he wrote of his 'steady, uniform, and essential friendship'
which had 'had for its object the improvement of my fortune
and respectability in life'. Similarly in 1813 he told Mr. Hamilton, 'You have uniformly been my best and most steady
friend. . . . You have, Sir, in a great many most essential and
important instances paved the way for me, and have enabled
me to better my circumstances.' Again, in 1817 he wrote, 'I
owe my success in life to your steady and friendly patronage';
and in 1820 he called Hamilton 'my first and best benefactor'.
Whatever his faults were, they did not include ingratitude.

He became a partner in Hunters & Company, and in his
early thirties began to play a part in the public life of his native
town. On 19 March 1792 he and five others were co-opted to
the Town Council of Maybole. About the same time, or a year
or two later, Niven had prospered enough to build himself a
new house on the south side of the High Street. Shortly afterwards he found a mistress for it, a girl named Isabella Christian
Goudie, whom he married in Glasgow on 9 September 1798.

Isabella was the daughter of the deceased Robert Goudie, of
Kingston, Jamaica. Here, probably, is the origin of the story
of the Jamaica fortune. But that rumour exaggerated it is
proved by the terms of William's and Isabella's marriage contract. All that he could settle on his bride was a free annuity
after his decease of £60 (which he later increased to £120), and
the liferent use of his house, furniture, and linen. Isabella herself had a tocher of only £800, and all that ultimately came to
her and her husband out of her father's estate was the sum of
£471 6s. 10d.[1]

There are other grounds too for doubting the legend of the
£100,000. Less than a year after his marriage, Niven bought

[1] Register of Deeds, vol. 739, pp. 250–4.

182

the farm of Kirkbride and two other small properties in the parish of Kirkmichael, some five miles south of Maybole, which had formed part of the Blairquhan estate and marched with that of Kilkerran. No legacy helped him to make this purchase. In fact he wrote rather doubtfully to Mr. Hamilton about 'making up the money necessary for the purchase which together with your kind assistance I hope I will get accomplished'.

Evidently it was something of an effort for him to buy Kirkbride. He completed the purchase, however, in June 1799—and in that month he had to borrow £3,000 from Hunters & Company, with 'the two merkland of Kirkbride' itself as security.[1]

It was probably at about the time of his marriage that he had his portrait painted. It shows a cautious face, with a long upper lip and a shrewd, tight mouth, such a countenance as might itself have given rise to the legend of parsimony.

Mrs. Niven lived till 15 February 1841,[2] her husband surviving nearly four years longer. There were no children of the marriage, and late in life Niven could entail his property only on his brother-in-law, John Goudie, who was then living with him, a grand-niece, and a distant cousin, 'Doctor Alexander Niven, late Minister of the Gospel at Dunkeld'.

During the Napoleonic wars Niven's business in Maybole was flourishing and he was playing a leading part in the Town Council, whose meetings he seldom missed. He did various kinds of business for his friend Mr. Hamilton of Pinmore, who in 1810, to Niven's great gratification, recommended him for appointment as one of the Deputy Lieutenants for Ayrshire.

Over the years he acquired considerable landed property, as is shown by the long list of it in his testamentary disposition of 3 September 1841.[3] He added to Kirkbride the farm of Auchalton 'with the lime rock therein', and it was presumably

[1] Ayr Sasines, xliii, ff. 217, 240, 409.
[2] Register of Deeds, vol. 739, p. 253.　　　　[3] Ibid., pp. 238–54.

he who worked the limestone quarry still to be seen some way above Auchalton beside the hill road, its shafts and galleries now fallen in and overgrown with whins and hawthorn. He also bought several small bits of land in and around Maybole, others on which part of the village of Crosshill was later built, and two or three farms in the distant parishes of Barr and Ballantrae.

In the very year of his death he was still buying land, and gave a bond for £7,000 for the farm of Threave in Kirkmichael parish. Besides land, his testament mentions furniture, plate, linen, china, and 'wines, spirits, and liquors of all kinds'.

Perhaps, like others who have raised themselves from humble beginnings to wealth and comfort, Niven provoked envy in some of his neighbours. That, I think, must have been the foundation of the tradition noted in Mr. Muir's book that 'he became hard and parsimonious to a degree'. For what evidence there is rather points the other way. Niven's testament, for instance, provided generous annuities to his factor and his servants, and in the whole document, the record of which runs to fifteen pages, there is nothing whatever suggestive of a miser. Moreover two writers in the *New Statistical Account of Scotland* make distinctly friendly allusions to Niven as an improver. One describes the estate of Kirkbride as having been 'a wild, bleak, barren moor' when he first took it in hand, but as so much improved by enclosures, planting, draining, liming, and the erection of 'elegant farm houses' as to give 'the pleasing impression of liberality on the part of the landlord, and domestic comfort on that of the tenant'.[1]

That was written in 1838. In the same year Niven was helping his philanthropic neighbour, Sir Charles Dalrymple Fergusson, who had just succeeded to the estate of Kilkerran, with the expense of building a chapel of ease (since erected into a parish church) for the new weaving village of Crosshill, whose houses had been built on land feued from both Kirkbride and Kilkerran. The implication of these activities is that Niven, far

---

[1] *New Statistical Account of Scotland*, Ayrshire, pp. 502–3.

from being parsimonious, was a man of generosity and public spirit.

Another favourable account of him appears in a contemporary description of Maybole:

'The town of Maybole has also of late been much improved. Access to it was formerly inconvenient and difficult, but, by the exertions of Mr. Niven of Kirkbride, who has always taken the greatest interest in the improvement of his native place, the streets have been opened by spacious roads to and from all quarters.'[1]

I possess one letter of Niven's which gives a glimpse of his road-making activities a quarter of a century before this time. Written on 28 July 1813, it shows that Niven had been busily promoting the extension of the by-road near Crosshill leading to Baird's Mill, to continue it for a further mile or so till it should join the road to Maybole constructed some twenty-two years earlier along the north-western slope of the Girvan valley. The project involved 190 'falls', four pends, and 'building the bridge and making a pend over the mill lade'. Niven had visited four other neighbouring lairds and fourteen farmers and procured subscriptions from them all, contributing five guineas himself—as much as anybody else except Mr. Thomas Francis Kennedy of Dunure who had put down ten. He had found some contractors, 'people in whom I have confidence', and got an estimate for the work. The sum so far subscribed would meet nearly two-thirds of the cost, and he now sent the estimate and subscription list to old Sir Adam Fergusson of Kilkerran (grand-uncle of the future Sir Charles), a notable improver in his time who had formerly made several miles of road in the Girvan valley. It was apparently he who had suggested the Baird's Mill road, since Niven expressed his hopes of its being completed 'to your satisfaction. . . . I trust,' he continued, 'you will not doubt that I used my best exertions,' and he respectfully invited Sir Adam 'to make up the balance'. Sir Adam readily agreed to subscribe twenty guineas, about

[1] *Ibid.*, p. 380.

half the balance: it was probably the last of his many contributions to the improvement of his countryside, for he died less than two months later, aged eighty. The rest of the money must have been raised, for the road was duly made and is in use today, though Baird's Mill is now a farm only.

Although he thus 'used his best exertions' as landowner and town councillor, Niven never became a magistrate of Maybole, as did his brother-in-law John Goudie in 1818. But in the first burgh election after the Reform Act, when town councils at last became popularly elected bodies, Niven was returned in a respectably high place on the list of successful candidates, despite having reached the ripe age of seventy-three. He remained on the council for another five years, and attended his last meeting on 14 October 1837. His death came seven years later.

It may be guessed that Niven had had dreams of founding a landed family. In his old age, when he had come to believe that his father, the Maybole shopkeeper, had been styled John Niven of Kirklandhill, he included in his testamentary disposition one clause in which vanity and disappointment are rather touchingly mingled. Any heir succeeding to his lands, he stipulated, must assume and retain 'the name, arms, and designation of Niven of Kirkbride'.

He had, in point of fact, no arms, although he had for many years been using a seal bearing the coat-of-arms of an old Shetland name, Niven of Shousburgh, with which he cannot possibly have had any kinship. He now took steps to obtain arms of his own, and registered them in the Lyon Office on 30 December 1842. They were basically the Shousburgh arms but differenced by 'three spears' heads in pale gules', evidently in allusion to the name of his mother, Janet Spear.

After his death on 13 December 1844, the Kirkbride estate passed to John Goudie, who duly assumed Niven as a middle name, and later to Niven's grand-niece Charlotte Hutcheson, only child of Hugh Hutcheson of Smithfield, Renfrewshire. She had married in 1832 Thomas Montgomery Cunninghame, who on his brother's death in 1846 became the eighth baronet of Corsehill and died in 1870. She survived till 1902 as 'the Dowager Lady Charlotte Montgomery Niven Cuninghame',[1] but with her death Niven's name died out. Her grandson, another Sir Thomas Montgomery Cuninghame, sold Kirkbride to its present owners.

Niven's portrait, by an unidentified artist, which was long at Kirkbride, was presented by Sir Thomas to the town council of Maybole about forty years ago, and is preserved in the town house. It has lately been cleaned and restored. His house in the High Street remains, appropriately, a bank.

[1] Thus in the Valuation Rolls for Carrick.

11

Baronet's Badge

'There is no title in the world,' observes Baptist Hatton, the learned antiquary in Disraeli's novel *Sybil*, 'for which I have such contempt as that of a baronet.'

He is addressing Sir Vavasour Firebrace, at this time the claimant to a peerage but figuring earlier in the story, in one of Disraeli's best satirical scenes, as the champion of the baronets, seeking 'their rights, their long withheld rights', the securing of which, in the age of Chartism, he seriously considers to be 'the question of the day'.

The rights of the baronets were once numerous and peculiar. A baronetcy is an hereditary form of knighthood, and as such is unique, but as an hereditary title of honour it is junior by some centuries to all others. Not only this, however, presumably aroused the contempt of Hatton the purist, but the circumstances of the title's inauguration. For in the first generation of its existence it was virtually offered for sale.

The privileges of the order, which King James VI decided in 1624 to extend to Scotland, were originally planned to attract support for a colonial scheme. The King had successfully founded the baronetage of England in 1611 and that of Ireland in 1619 as a means to finance the plantation of Ulster. The first baronets had received their honours on each paying a sum equal to £1,100 into the Exchequer, which between 1611 and 1622 had benefited from these creations to the extent of £225,000.

These first baronets had been English country gentlemen,

188

and candidates for the order were expected to possess land of an annual rental of at least £1,000. The King now hoped that Scottish gentlemen might in a similar way be induced to assist in developing the colony of Nova Scotia or 'New Scotland', the large and imperfectly defined territory across the Atlantic Ocean which he had granted to Sir William Alexander of Menstrie—poet, statesman, and the first Scottish imperialist. The suggestion of extending the baronetage to Scotland for this purpose apparently came from Sir William himself.[1]

The King wrote to the Scottish Privy Council on 18 October 1624 announcing his intention to confer the new honour 'upoun suche as were worthie of that degree, and will agree for ane proportioun of ground within New Scotland'. He invited the Council's advice towards the furthering of 'this so worthie worke'.[2]

The Council received the royal letter on 4 November, and after deliberation issued in the King's name on 30 November a proclamation defining the new order's privileges and obligations, and inviting applicants for it—who had to be 'knichts and gentlemen of cheife respect for ther birth, place, or fortounes'—to send in their names by 1 April. Candidates for the honour were to engage themselves 'to sett furth sex sufficient men, artificeris or labourers, sufficientlie armeit, apparrellit, and victuallit for tua yearis, towards his Majesteis royal colonie', and also to undertake to pay to Sir William Alexander, who had been appointed the King's Lieutenant for the colony, a sum of 1,000 merks for his 'past chargeis in discoverie of the said cuntrey' and for such interest in it as he was to surrender to them.[3] But it must have proved very difficult to find workmen willing to leave their employment in Scotland to go to a completely unknown country on what would have seemed to them like the other side of the world, and the obligation to provide six artificers or labourers was soon dropped. The following

[1] Rev. Charles Rogers, *Memorials of . . . the House of Alexander*, i, pp. 68–70.

[2] *Privy Council Register*, xiii, pp. 616–17. [3] *Ibid.*, pp. 625, 633–4.

March a letter from King James allowed the subscription of 2,000 merks alone as an alternative, if preferred, to 1,000 merks and six men.[1] The letter was probably authorized by his son, for the old King was by now on his death-bed. He expired four days after its date, before it had reached Edinburgh and before a single Scottish baronet had been created.

Such were the obligations. The following were the privileges, which, as will be explained, came to exceed those of the Ulster baronets. The Nova Scotia baronets, who were to be limited to the number of 100 (later increased to 150), were promised place and precedence after the younger sons of peers and before all knights (except those created by the King upon a battle-field), before all *barones minores* (lairds holding directly of the Crown in free barony), and before all esquires and gentlemen. They were to have a special addition to their coat-of-arms, station next to the Royal standard in battle, and the word 'Sir' prefixed and the style and title of 'Baronet' subjoined to their names. Their wives were to be styled Lady, Madam, and Dame. Further, the dignity of a knight baronet, unlike ordinary knighthood, was to descend to heirs male.

With these honours, much the same as those granted to the English and Irish baronets, each Scottish baronet was to receive an estate in Nova Scotia, held of the King, the size of which was later fixed at 16,000 acres, on which he would be able to do almost anything he liked, from mining for gold and silver to founding a burgh of barony.

King James and Sir William Alexander had hoped that the new scheme would be popular. The Privy Council's proclamation had frankly recommended it as 'ane fitt, warrandable, and convenient means to disburding this his Majesties said ancient kingdome of all such younger brether and meane gentlemen quhois moyens ar short of thair birth, worth, or myndis, who otherwayes most be troublesome to the houssis and freinds from whence they ar descendit (the common ruynes of most of the ancient families), or betak thameselffis

[1] *Privy Council Register*, xiii, pp. 721–2.

190

to forren warre or baisser chifts'.[1] The new King, Charles I, was already interested in his father's scheme and took it up warmly. The first eight baronets of Nova Scotia were created on 28 and 29 May, less than two months after his accession, and Sir William's charter of Nova Scotia was confirmed two months later. But the project did not arouse the response that the King or his late father had hoped for.

The applicants were disappointingly few, even from among those 'younger brether and meane gentlemen' with 'moyens' unequal to their birth or pretensions whom it had been specially hoped to attract. No one seemed anxious to get rid of his poor relations. No one knew anything of the remote land where the new estates and baronies were to be. It was as if the baronets had been given proprietorships in the moon. Moreover knights, barons and gentlemen resented the insertion between them and the nobility of the precedence promised to the baronets; and on 2 November 1625 the Estates, by a majority, supported a petition from them against it.[2] The reply to this was a royal proclamation dated 12 February 1626 coldly warning 'the said gentrie that they may ather procure the said dignitie for them selffis or not repyne at others for doeing the same'. The proclamation also offered a further inducement to potential applicants, which had been a privilege of the Ulster baronets since 1612. The Chancellor of Scotland was authorized to bestow knighthood on the eldest sons of baronets as soon as they reached the age of twenty-one, 'he being requyred to that effect'.[3]

Yet still, for one reason or another, nothing like 100 suitable candidates appeared. By the end of 1627 only thirty-five baronets had received their patents, and by 1638 still only ninety-one, even though, in default of Scots, patents had been bestowed on several Englishmen and Irishmen, two Frenchmen, and even one woman, with remainder to her heirs male.

[1] *Ibid.*, p. 649.   [2] *Acts of the Parliament of Scotland*, v, pp. 184, 187–8.
[3] *Royal Letters, Charters, and Tracts relating to . . . Nova Scotia* (Bannatyne Club), pp. 31–2.

So other attractions were offered. The baronets need not journey to London to receive their patents but might procure them in Edinburgh; the fees claimed by the heralds were, by royal command, waived; and in 1629 the baronets of Nova Scotia, 'that they may be the better knowne and distinguished from other persouns', were given the right to wear round their necks on an orange-tawny ribbon a badge with the arms of Nova Scotia and the motto of Henry, Prince of Wales, the King's deceased brother—*Fax mentis honestae gloria*. The other baronets had no badge till 300 years later. (It was a sore point with Sir Vavasour Firebrace.) Finally, these proffered privileges being still undervalued, it was ordained that persons usurping the precedence or cognisance of a baronet should be fined and imprisoned; and in 1633 all the privileges of Nova Scotia baronets were ratified by Act of Parliament.

But by this time estates in Nova Scotia had become more than ever like fairy gold. In 1631 King Charles had ceded Nova Scotia to the French, and the colony was no longer Scottish territory. With typical lack of candour he promised the baronets to maintain all their rights there, and continued to grant charters for baronies in Nova Scotia up to 1637. When Charles II revived the order, baronets received patents without charters, and no longer had to pay for them. One baronetcy created by Charles II, that of Dalyell of the Binns, passes, by a special remainder, through the female line, remaining dormant till a male succeeds. The succession to the baronetcy of Maxwell of Pollok, also created by him in 1682, was extended, by another patent from Queen Anne in 1707, to heirs of tailzie. But the usual succession of Novia Scotia baronetcies is to heirs male of the body of the first holder.

Every baronet created under the Great Seal of Scotland— that is, down to the Union of 1707—was a baronet of Nova Scotia; and since with each generation the number of possible heirs tends to increase, not very many Nova Scotia baronetcies have died out, though many have become merged in peerages. There are still about 100 baronets of Nova Scotia who are not peers; and more than twenty of these are the successors of ancestors who once legally possessed though they never actually saw a Nova Scotia estate.

One such ancestor was Sir Thomas Burnett of Leys, who was granted the estate of Leyis-Burnet in New Scotland on 21 April 1626.[1] Among the Burnett family muniments preserved in the lovely old Deeside tower of Crathes may be seen, in fine condition, the disposition to him signed by Sir William Alexander (and witnessed by his friend and fellow-poet William Drummond of Hawthornden), the huge charter with the Great Seal of King Charles I attached, and the instrument recording that sasine of Leyis-Burnet was given to Sir Thomas on the Castle Hill of Edinburgh.

This last document deserves a footnote. There is a popular belief, still voiced on occasion by Edinburgh publicists, that the Castle Hill was declared to be, and still today legally remains, a part of Nova Scotia. This is erroneous. The early baronets' charters merely provided that sasine—the formal presentation to the new owner of earth and stone, essential in every transfer of land down to 1845—should be given on the Castle Hill as a convenient spot. The precept following or contained in any charter directed sasine to be given at some particular point of the property to be conveyed, usually at the principal 'messuage' or dwelling-house. In this case, for obvious convenience, it was to be given in the old country instead of in the new where the estate lay, and the designated spot was 'at our castle of Edinburgh as the most eminent and principal place of our said kingdom of Scotland'.

A bronze tablet was placed near the main gate of Edinburgh Castle in 1953 and unveiled by the Premier of Nova Scotia to commemorate these ceremonies of more than three centuries ago.

After the Usurpation several of the peculiar privileges of Scottish baronets fell, as lawyers say, into desuetude. But the

[1] His present heir, being also possessed of a U.K. baronetcy, has not claimed the baronetcy of Burnett of Leys.

rights of designation and of precedence have continued to the present day; and one distinctive privilege was, after a lapse of some generations, revived, and has continued to be maintained on formal occasions ever since. This was the right to wear the badge with the arms of Nova Scotia and the Prince's motto, on its orange-tawny ribbon, granted in 1629.

The practice of wearing the badge 'fell to the ground, with all the other honours of Scotland, during the usurpation of the Long Parliament, and of Oliver Cromwell: it continued in general, though not total disuse, at the Restoration'.[1] There was an attempt to re-introduce it in 1725, suggested by the revival of the Order of the Bath in that year, and another in 1734. But a more determined and in fact an effective one was made in 1775.

The initiative came from the office of the Lord Lyon King of Arms, but a letter of 1777 from James Cummyng, keeper of the Lyon Office records, who was intimately concerned with the whole business, implies that the original suggestion arose from Charles, tenth Lord Elphinstone, whose interest must have been quite altruistic since he held no baronetcy himself. 'The whole Order,' wrote Mr. Cummyng, 'are under the greatest obligations to Lord Elphinstone who has been extremely active in calling their attention to this great object.'[2] But the circular letter to all the Nova Scotia baronets which really began the movement came from the Lyon-Depute, Robert Boswell, dated 30 March 1775. 'As by the nature of my office,' he wrote, 'I am called upon to attend to the observance of regularity and propriety in all matters of honour, I think it proper to remind you, as a Baronet of Scotland, of the privilege of your Order'.[3]

The circular letter was well received, and as a result two meetings of baronets of Nova Scotia were held; one in London

---

[1] William Playfair, *British Family Antiquity, vol. viii, containing the Baronetage of Scotland*, p. xxix.
[2] Yule MSS (Register House), sec. 2, No. 246.
[3] Playfair, *op. cit.*, Appendix, p. 24.

at the British Coffee House, near Charing Cross, a favourite place of resort over many years for Scotsmen in London, and the other at Fortune's Tavern in Edinburgh. The latter, on 14 June, was more than a fortnight after the former, and was fortified by assurances of support from the baronets in London. At Fortune's Tavern twenty-one baronets attended, with proxies from six more, and letters of support were read from twenty-five others. Some of those present had brought with them and displayed to the meeting original badges which had belonged to their ancestors. The assembled baronets unanimously resolved to resume the wearing of the badge, and appointed a committee, with Mr. Cummyng as its secretary, to communicate their resolution to other Nova Scotia baronets and to the Secretary of State for the Northern Department. The committee were also to get badges made, 'under the inspection of the Lyon Court', on the model of those exhibited at the meeting. Finally the baronets resolved 'to write a letter of thanks to the Lord-Lyon for his attention to the honour of his country'.

On 28 June Sir James Cockburn of that ilk, Usher of the White Rod,[1] called on the Secretary of State (the Earl of Suffolk), accompanied by such Scottish baronets as he could find in London, to inform him officially of the meeting's resolutions; and on 30 June Mr. Cummyng sent out another circular to all the Nova Scotia baronets. This enclosed an engraving showing the proper form of the badge and asked each recipient to state whether he would like to have one made for him and whether he would 'chuse any embellishments in jewels, as several gentlemen do'. A few weeks later Mr. Cummyng announced that he was about to set out for Birmingham to order the badges there. It seems strange that no jeweller competent to make them was apparently to be found in Edinburgh.

[1] Sir James had received sasine of the office of heritable Usher to His Majesty in Scotland, with a salary of £250 a year, on 12 May 1768 (General Register of Sasines, vol. 269, ff. 163–6).

It was decided that the baronets should take as the first occasion of wearing their badges the 25th of October following, which was the anniversary of the King's accession. On St. Andrews's Day several Nova Scotia baronets in London 'went to Court in their proper insignia, and were graciously received'.[1] Thus the revived practice was both established and approved. The badge is still worn today on all occasions when 'orders and decorations' are specified, with either uniform or civilian dress.

It was not at once adopted after its revival by all entitled to do so. But from 1775 onwards it was gradually taken up, and the Nova Scotia badge makes a fairly frequent appearance in Scottish portraits of the age of Reynolds, Raeburn and their followers. In these the orange-tawny ribbon is much in evidence, of such length that the badge hangs low on the wearer's breast, sometimes almost to his waist. But in modern times it has been worn, like the badges of other orders of knighthood, on a short ribbon, hanging just below the collar.

The distinction was regarded with no little envy by the baronets of England, Ireland, Great Britain, and the United Kingdom. After a long agitation they at length, in 1929, secured from King George V a Royal Warrant permitting them to wear a badge, though of course with a different device thereon (the arms of Ulster), no motto, and the orange-tawny ribbon differenced by a dark-blue edge. Disraeli's satire was prophetic when he represented Sir Vavasour Firebrace, (who demanded for himself and his brethren, among other distinctions, a coronet 'of two balls', a thumb-ring, and a collar of SS) as mourning that, but for the untimely death of King William IV, 'we should at least have had the badge'.

But Disraeli's model for Sir Vavasour was in fact a Scotsman, Mr. Richard Broun, afterwards Sir Richard Broun of Colstoun, eighth baronet. In 1836 he claimed knighthood as a baronet's eldest son—probably the last man to do so; but his claim, after reference to the College of Arms (not, as would surely have

[1] Playfair, *op. cit.*, Appendix, p. 26.

9. Baronet's badge

been more appropriate, to the Lyon Office), was refused.[1] He also organized a meeting of baronets in Edinburgh, whose demands, none of which was granted, included all Sir Vavasour Firebrace's and even more.

[1] See a curious pamphlet, *The Case of the Honourable the Baronets of Scotland and Nova Scotia* (Edinburgh, 1836), which Disraeli must certainly have read.

12

'*A Pair of Butts*'

As we today, in estimating short distances, often use illustrations drawn from sport, so did our forefathers of Stewart and early Hanoverian times. As we cite the length of a cricket-pitch, a tennis-court, a football-field, or a 'mashie shot', so they sometimes spoke of 'a pennystone cast' —referring to a game something like ducks-and-drakes—and, more commonly, when estimating a longer distance, of 'a butt-length' or 'a pair of butts'.

The figure of 'a pair of butts' is drawn from archery, and its common use all over Scotland is to be attributed to the fact that, in accordance with the law, a pair of butts used to stand near each parish church, a familiar object to every parishioner. The well-known statute of 1424 enacted by the first Parliament of James I after his return from his English captivity to enforce the practice of archery throughout his realm was reinforced by another of James II in 1457 ordaining the holding of wapin-schaws, the discouragement of football and golf, and the making of 'at ilk paroch kirk a paire of buttis', where regular practice, under pain of a fine, was to be 'usyt ilk Sunday'.[1]

Parliament did not specify who was to be responsible for the upkeep of the butts in rural parishes, and they were probably never very well maintained. But in towns the town councils were clearly responsible; and references to building or repairing butts are fairly common in the records of the royal burghs. At Peebles it was the custom to earmark the 'burgess silver' paid

---

[1] *A.P.S.*, ii, pp. 6, 48.

by newly admitted burgesses for 'the makyn of the buttis', and such expenditure is noted as early as 1464. The 'bow buttis' of Peebles were still maintained in the reign of Charles I, the silver arrow, for which the Royal Company of Archers still compete, being first shot for there in 1628.[1] There is a similar record in the Dundee accounts on 4 April 1521, when the Provost and Bailies 'grantit to Robyn Huyd'—an appropriate name—'to the bigging of the butts a burgess-ship or five merks of money'; and at St. Andrews in the early eighteenth century the St. Leonard's College butts were kept in repair at the students' expense.[2] The burgh accounts of Ayr record many disbursements for building or repairing the town butts between 1541–2 and 1612–13.[3] The Dumbarton butts are mentioned in the Lord Treasurer's Accounts in 1498, because King James IV, a keen archer, 'tint' thirty-five shillings there; and references to the town butts of Stirling, apart from the private royal butts which the same monarch had made by his gardener 'furth of the garding beside the stable', extend over a very long period from the time when the King 'tint' seven shillings at them in 1497.[4] In 1561 the Stirling town council 'grantit that the thesaurair big and reform ane pair of buttis in the yarde sumtyme callit the Grayfreir yarde apone the townes expens'; and generations later, when archery had become a peaceful pastime only, their successors appointed the payment 'to George Monro, merchand, in name of the society of archers in this place', the sum of £35 2s. Scots 'debursed by him in building the butts and making ane entry thereto'.[5]

When the town or parish butts fell into disuse, they remained a landmark; and when even their remains disappeared under

[1] *Peebles Burgh Records*, p. 151; Robert Renwick, *The Burgh of Peebles*, pp. 80, 97.

[2] Alexander Maxwell, *Old Dundee*, pp. 260–1; Dickinson, *Two Students at St. Andrews, 1711–1716*, p. xxxvi.

[3] *Ayr Burgh Accounts* (Scottish History Society), pp. 89, 112, 122, 146, 154, 163, 178, 255.

[4] *Treasurer's Accounts*, ii, pp. 390, 448, 329.

[5] *Stirling Burgh Records, 1519–1666*, p. 78; *ibid.*, 1667–1752, p. 210.

the plough or the foundations of houses, the name, in many places, survived to indicate if not a precise spot at least a well-known area, as with Newington Butts, once outside London. At St. Andrews and Haddington, 'the Butts' still means something to every resident. At Glasgow, a minor but decisive battle took place on 24 May 1544 on the ground of the town butts 'upoun the muir of Glasgow, ane myle from the citie apoun the eist pairte thairof', when the Governor Arran encountered the Earl of Glencairn and his party, consisting of the barons and lairds of Renfrewshire and the Lennox and the 'haill burgesses' of Glasgow, and worsted them after a bitter fight.[1] This engagement became traditionally known as 'the battle of the Butts', and has indeed no other name.[2]

Traditional sites of butts were also long pointed out near Renfrew and in the parishes of Glencairn in Dumfriesshire and Strachan in Kincardineshire; and at Dunfermline part of the burgh's common lands was known as the Lammer Butts.[3]

The expression 'a pair of butts' is as orthodox as 'a pair of breeches' or 'a pair of scissors'. Butts were and are built in pairs, one at each end of the shooting-ground, so as to allow shooting from each end of the range alternately. 'A paire of buttis' is the term used in the 1457 Act already quoted. It was 'ane paire of buttis' that the town council of Stirling ordered in 1561, or the town council of Edinburgh in 1610 directed their treasurer 'to big . . . to the scholares of the hie schole besyde the same at the toun wall'.[4] In 1708 the Royal Company of Archers agreed with John Monro 'to putt up a pair of new butts'; in 1715 the town council of Edinburgh allowed them to erect 'a new pair of butts' on ground lying on the west side of the Parliament House; and in 1726 Mr. Thomas Hope of Ran-

[1] John Lesley, *The History of Scotland* (Bannatyne Club), p. 176; *Diurnal of Occurrents* pp. 32–3.

[2] *New Statistical Account*, vi (Lanark), p. 109; Renwick and Lindsay, *History of Glasgow*, ii, p. 369.

[3] *Burgh Records of Dunfermline*, p. 55.

[4] *Extracts from the Records of the Burgh of Edinburgh*, p. 60.

keillour offered them 'a piece of ground in Hope Park . . . sufficient for a pair of butts, to be built and repaired upon the charge of the Royal Company'.[1] The statutory phrase thus runs through the whole history of Scottish archery.

It is, however, as a topographical measurement that the phrase most commonly occurs, sometimes varied into 'a butt-length'. Instances in *Macfarlane's Geographical Collections*,[2] far too many to enumerate here, show the phrase still in regular use in the first quarter of the eighteenth century. But it was evidently current in colloquial speech very much earlier. One instance occurs in a famous passage of John Knox's *History of the Reformation* when he describes the foggy weather prevailing when Mary Queen of Scots landed at Leith on 19 August 1561—'The myst was so thick and so dark, that skairse mycht any man espy ane other the lenth of two pair of buttis.'[3]

But what shows the natural and instinctive use of the phrase best of all is its occurrence in the mouths of witnesses when judicially examined as to precise distances. Men are described, or describe themselves, as approaching to 'the space of ane pair of buttis' (1569),[4] or 'returnand fra the said place towardis Edinburgh be the space of two pair of butlenthis' (1580),[5] or 'besetting' somebody 'within tua pair of butt lenths' (1596);[6] the distance of one house from another is reckoned as 'the speace of sax pair of buttis' (1621), or a man offers an alibi— 'that he was . . . not present at the delyvrie, and in the mean time was within 4 or 5 pair of but of the house' (1684).[7] Two examples of the phrase occur in the evidence led during the inquiry by the Lords of the Articles into the 'conspiracy' at Gowrie House in 1600. The Duke of Lennox deponed that King James VI was met by the Earl of Gowrie 'as his majestie

---

[1] Balfour Paul, *The History of the Royal Company of Archers*, pp. 255–7.

[2] 3 vols. (Scottish History Society).

[3] Knox's *Works* (ed. Laing), ii, p. 26.

[4] *Privy Council Register*, ii, p. 38.   [5] *Ibid.*, iii, p. 290.

[6] *Highland Papers* (Scottish History Society), i, p. 193.

[7] *Privy Council Register*, xii, p. 415. *Chronicles of the Atholl and Tullibardine Families*, i, pp. 193–4.

wes within tua pair of butelangis of the towne of Perth'; and
the Abbot of Lindores, describing the agitated scene outside
Gowrie House just after the King had bawled for help from the
tower window, affirmed that 'the erle of Gowrie . . . incontinent
ran the space of half ane pair of butlandis frome thame
towardis Glenurquhyis house'.[1] The last quotation gives a rare
instance of using the butt-length fractionally.

The phrase has been heard, too, in the Court of Session, for
example when the precise measurement of distance was a
fundamental point concerning a man's physical capacity. Lord
Harcarse wrote:

'In a reduction *ex capite lecti* of a disposition made by one
Craigengelt to John Keiry's son, at the instance of the dis-
poner's heir; It was alledged for the defender: That the defunct
did posterior acts of health equivalent to the going to kirk and
market, *viz.* he came a pair of butts out of his house unsupported to a coach, wherein he travelled six miles to Alloway,
and walked up two pair of stairs to John Keiry's house, and
did several other domestic acts.'[2]

A similar case had been earlier noted by Lord Stair:

'In the case Clellands *contra* Clelland of Faskin, the defunct
finding that his disposition was quarrelld and stopped at the
Exchequer, as being done *in lecto*, immediately after he caused
make a chair, with a fixed footstool to bear his feet, in which he
was carried with men till he came within two pair or thereby to
the kirk, and thence he walked to the kirk, but there was no
congregation, and returned back to the chair, and so was
carried home. . . . In Clellands case, his going several times to
his barn, and to some trees a pair from his gate unsupported,
were not found equivalent to going to kirk and market.'[3]

These quotations from Stair are of special interest as show-

[1] *A.P.S.*, iv, pp. 203–7.

[2] Sir Roger Hog of Harcarse, *Decisions of the Court of Session, from
1681 to 1691* (1757), p. 189.

[3] Sir James Dalrymple of Stair, *The Institutions of the Law of Scotland*
(1681), Part II, pp. 96, 97.

ing how in course of time the familiar phrase came to be abbreviated into simply 'a pair'. In Stair's second edition of 1693 (p. 445) the same term is used in both passages; but in the third edition of 1759 (pp. 464, 465) the eighteenth-century editor thought it advisable to add the words '*of butts*', an indication that the once common expression was being forgotten. It seems indeed to have passed out of currency about the middle of the eighteenth century, and is today so far forgotten that two modern editors of Knox's *History of the Reformation* have taken 'butts' in the passage quoted above to mean 'boots'.[1]

For some 300 years, none the less, the phrase 'a pair of butts' meant to the ordinary Scotsman a short and definite distance which he could immediately visualize. Yet today the question must be asked—how short, or how long, was it?

To begin with, it is clear that a butt-length was something different from another estimate of distance, a bowshot or bowdraught, and in fact shorter. In a description of the islands in Loch Lomond, apparently taken from notes made by Timothy Pont, the terms 'a pair of butts long', 'a pair of butts of lenth', and '2 pair butts long' obviously indicate different measurements from 'a bow shot long', 'a bow draught', and 'thrie flight shot', which appear in the same account.[2] Elsewhere, for example, it is observed that the town of Lauder 'stands about a bowdraught be west the water',[3] or that (in 1577) a ship 'lay opoun hir ankir, neirby the schoir on the eist syde within half ane flicht schot to land'.[4]

A bowdraught or a flight shot evidently meant the full range of an arrow aimed with a high trajectory, not the shorter distance which an ordinary citizen was expected to reach every

---

[1] *The Historie of the Reformation . . . by John Knox: a Selection*, ed. Ralph S. Walker (Saltire Society), 1940, p. 58; *John Knox's History of the Reformation in Scotland*, ed. W. Croft Dickinson, 1949, ii, p. 7; cp. i, p. 106.

[2] *Macfarlane's Geographical Collections*, ii, pp. 602–4.

[3] *Ibid.*, iii, p. 174.   [4] *Privy Council Register*, ii, p. 654.

Sunday afternoon. It would be, at the most, assuming a very heavy bow, some 300 yards. One of the best archers in the Royal Company today tells me that he has never shot an arrow further than 220 yards; and the greatest range at which the Royal Company compete in target-shooting is 200 yards. The butt-length, then, was considerably shorter.

The Royal Company's butts measure only 30 yards; and the Kilwinning town butts measured in the eighteenth century only 26 yards, but shooting for prizes at that range was termed '*point-blank* distance' and evidently regarded as below the normal.[1] The Earl of Gowrie's run of half a pair of butts would not have been thought worth so describing had it been only 13 or 15 yards; nor would a race 'betuix the buttis' at Stirling in 1502 have been, if only 30 yards or less, worth a wager by King James IV.[2]

I believe the statutory butt-length in Scotland to have been 120 yards, of which the 30-yard range is one quarter. The relationship between the two is made clear by an authoritative work on archery published more than a century ago:

'The moderns have not departed from the old fashion, except that our butts, like those who use them, are rather more precise. . . . They are arranged in sets. . . . One hundred and twenty yards being measured, a but of ten feet broad, eighteen inches wide at the top, and about six feet in height, is erected at the two extremities. Thirty yards distant from one of these, and a little to the right hand, they place a second; sixty yards to the left, a third, and ninety to the right, a fourth; which forms a complete set, no one of which impedes the view of the others.'[3]

It is most probable that the statutory pair of butts, though intended to be 'precise', was not always so. Certainly when used as an estimate of distance it is often qualified, not merely

---

[1] *Statistical Account of Scotland*, xi, p. 174.

[2] *Treasurer's Accounts*, ii, p. 149.

[3] G. A. Hansard, *The Book of Archery* (1840), pp. 110–11. I owe this illuminating quotation to Mr. Robert Scarlett of Sweethope.

by some hesitant phrase like 'about the length of a butt' or 'a pair of butts or more' but by extensions such as 'about two large pair of butts', in the same tone as the estimate 'about two good bowdraughts', or as references to 'short miles' and 'long miles'.

The question could be definitely settled by the discovery and measurement of a genuine surviving pair of medieval or even seventeenth-century butts. Meanwhile a few of the conjectural distances recorded in Macfarlane's *Collections* can be checked. Two estimates in the parish of Airth, for example, one of 'about two large pair of butts' and the other of 'about two pair of butts' accord with a normal butt-length of something well over 100 yards.[1] Again, in an account of the parish of Bothkennar in Stirlingshire occurs the sentence, 'Two large pair of butts west from the kirk stands the house of Westertown upon the northside of Carron.'[2] This distance is precisely 277 yards, not much more than the 240 yards which a simple 'two pair of butts' would have been.

[1] *Macfarlane's Geographical Collections*, i, pp. 327, 329.
[2] *Ibid.*, i, p. 325.

Index